Private Equity Horizons: Navigating Opportunities and Shaping the Future

Alex Thompson

Published by Side Hustle Success, 2023.

PRIVATE EQUITY HORIZONS: NAVIGATING OPPORTUNITIES AND SHAPING THE FUTURE

First edition. October 2, 2023.

ISBN: 979-8223538950

Written by Alex Thompson.

Also by Alex Thompson

Alex on Finance

Financial Freedom Roadmap - Achieving Early Retirement through the FIRE Movement

The Art of Strategic Innovation

Beyond Cash - The Evolution of Digital Payment Systems and the Future of Money

Preserving Wealth in Inflationary Times - Strategies for Protecting Your Financial Future

Standalone

Side Hustle Success: Unlocking Your Entrepreneurial Potential

Side Hustle Success: The Ultimate Guide to Passive and Financial Freedom

Mastering the Markets: Advanced Trading Strategies for Success and Ethical Trading Practices

Financial Fortitude

Mastering the Art of Upselling

The Financial Bullet Blueprint

Investing Demystified: A Beginner's Guide to Building Wealth in the Stock Market

Real Estate Riches: Building Wealth through Property Investment

How To Succeed as a Freelancer

Navigating Complex Waters: Advanced Strategies in Portfolio Management
Behavioral Finance and Investor Psychology
Leading with Empathy: Harnessing Emotional Intelligence for Effective Leadership
Financial Independence
Thriving Within Your Means: A Guide to Affordable Living
Algorithmic Trading: Navigating the Digital Frontier
Navigating Alternative Investments
Navigating the Behavioral Finance Landscape
Unlocking the Power of Derivatives
Mastering International Finance
Quantitative Finance and Risk Modeling
Sustainable and ESG Investing
Derivatives Dynamics: Navigating Risk and Innovation
Options Mastery: Navigating the Financial Frontier
Portfolio Mastery: Navigating the Financial Art and Science
Ethics in Hedge Funds: Navigating the Moral Compass of Finance
Structured Finance: Navigating Innovation, Sustainability and Ethics
Commodity Trading: Navigating Markets, Sustainability, and Innovation
Ethical Valuation: Navigating the Future of Startup Investments
Navigating Financial Risk: Strategies for a Dynamic World
Navigating the New Frontier: Understanding Market Microstructure in the Digital Age
Mastering Mergers and Acquisitions: Strategies, Successes and Lessons
Mastering Real Estate Investment: Strategies, Trends and Success Stories
Navigating Investor Behavior: Insights from Behavioral Finance
Private Equity Horizons: Navigating Opportunities and Shaping the Future

Table of Contents

Dedicated to all the professionals, visionaries, and investors who passionately contribute to the growth and evolution of private equity. Your dedication and innovation shape the industry's future and inspire others to embrace the exciting possibilities that lie ahead.

Chapter 1: Introduction to Private Equity

Understanding Private Equity Investments

In the realm of finance and business, private equity investments represent a dynamic and influential force. These investments, unlike their publicly traded counterparts, hold unique characteristics and significance within the financial landscape. This section takes us on a journey to explore the fundamental principles of private equity, shedding light on what defines this investment class and its multifaceted nature.

Defining Private Equity: At its core, private equity investments involve the allocation of capital to non-publicly traded companies. Unlike public equity, which finds its home on stock exchanges, private equity operates in the realm of closely held businesses. Within this sphere, investors, often in the form of pooled funds or specialized firms, seek to acquire equity stakes in private enterprises. These investments collectively form a distinctive asset class, characterized by a distinct set of rules and expectations.

Investment Structure: Central to the world of private equity is its unique investment structure. Funds or firms specializing in this asset class gather capital from an array of investors, ranging from institutional giants to individual high-net-worth individuals and even endowments. This capital serves as the lifeblood of private equity endeavors, fueling the acquisition of ownership interests in privately held companies.

Investment Horizon: A defining characteristic of private equity investments lies in their extended investment horizon. Unlike the rapid fluctuations and daily trading of public equity markets, private equity takes a longer view. It is not uncommon for these investments to span several years, with a focus on creating sustainable value over the long term. This extended engagement often includes active participation in the management and operations of portfolio companies, setting it apart from more transient forms of investment.

Types of Private Equity: Private equity encompasses a diverse array of investment strategies, each with its unique objectives and risk profiles. These strategies include venture capital, buyouts, growth capital, distressed asset acquisition, and more. Each approach tailors its focus to specific investment opportunities and market conditions, allowing for adaptability and strategic maneuvering.

Risk and Return: Private equity investments offer the potential for substantial returns. However, they also carry elevated risks and a degree of illiquidity compared to publicly traded securities. Investors willingly embrace these risks in pursuit of the potentially higher rewards, recognizing the need for compensation commensurate with the challenges they entail.

Value Creation: A defining aspect of private equity lies in its proactive approach to value creation. Private equity investors actively engage with their portfolio companies, working to enhance their overall value. This involves strategic initiatives, operational improvements, cost management, and expansion strategies that collectively contribute to the growth and profitability of the underlying businesses.

Exit Strategies: Realizing returns on private equity investments typically involves carefully planned exit strategies. These strategies may include taking portfolio companies public through initial public offerings (IPOs), executing secondary sales, or selling the companies to other investors or strategic buyers. The choice of exit strategy depends on market conditions and the specific goals of the investment.

Role in Capital Markets: Private equity plays a vital role in fostering entrepreneurship, innovation, and job creation. It serves as an alternative source of capital for businesses beyond traditional debt and public equity markets. By providing funding and expertise to promising enterprises, private equity contributes to the dynamism and diversity of the corporate landscape.

Regulatory Framework: The world of private equity is subject to regulatory oversight in various jurisdictions. Regulations aim to safeguard the interests of investors and maintain market integrity. Understanding the regulatory landscape is crucial for both investors and private equity firms to operate within legal boundaries.

Global Reach: Private equity is a global industry, with investments and transactions transcending international borders. It often involves a diverse array of investors and companies from different parts of the world. The global reach of private equity highlights its adaptability to varying market conditions and its potential to facilitate cross-border economic activity.

Understanding Private Equity Investments

To truly appreciate the world of private equity, it's essential to delve into its historical evolution. Private equity's roots reach deep into the annals of financial history, where its growth and development have been marked by significant milestones. In this section, we explore the rich historical tapestry that has shaped private equity into the dynamic and influential asset class it is today.

Ancient Beginnings: The early seeds of private equity can be traced back to ancient civilizations, where wealthy individuals and families would provide capital to support various enterprises. These early forms of private equity were often characterized by direct investments in private companies, helping fund expansion, innovation, and entrepreneurial ventures.

Early Venture Capital: The mid-20th century saw the emergence of venture capital as a distinct form of private equity. This era witnessed the birth of Silicon Valley, where venture capitalists played a pivotal role in nurturing innovative startups. Their investments not only provided capital but also valuable mentorship and guidance to visionary entrepreneurs.

The Era of Leveraged Buyouts (LBOs): The 1960s and 1970s marked a transformative phase for private equity with the rise of leveraged buyouts (LBOs). During this period, private equity firms began acquiring publicly traded companies, often utilizing significant debt. The objective was to unlock value through operational improvements, cost efficiencies, and strategic restructuring.

Regulatory Shifts: The 1980s brought about regulatory changes that supported the growth of private equity. Reforms like the Tax Reform Act of 1986 in the United States facilitated the formation of private equity partnerships and incentivized investments in privately held companies.

Institutionalization of Private Equity: By the late 20th century, private equity had gained recognition as a distinct asset class. Institutional investors such as pension funds and endowments started allocating substantial capital to private equity funds. This institutionalization of private equity led to the establishment of larger and more diversified funds.

Global Expansion: The 21st century witnessed the globalization of private equity. Firms expanded their reach beyond national borders, engaging in cross-border investments and transactions. This global perspective allowed private equity to become a significant player in international finance.

Diverse Investment Strategies: Today, private equity encompasses a wide spectrum of investment strategies. These range from venture capital, aimed at early-stage startups, to growth capital for expanding businesses, buyouts of mature companies, distressed asset acquisition, and mezzanine financing. This diversity of strategies showcases private equity's ability to adapt to varying market conditions and seize diverse investment opportunities.

Technological Advancements: Recent years have seen the integration of technological advancements into the private equity landscape. Data analytics, artificial intelligence, and digital platforms have become indispensable tools for due diligence, investment analysis, and portfolio management.

Challenges and Innovation: Throughout its history, private equity has faced various challenges, including economic downturns, regulatory shifts, and changing market dynamics. However, these challenges have also spurred innovation and adaptation within the industry, reinforcing its resilience and ability to evolve.

Understanding the historical evolution of private equity offers essential context for comprehending its current dynamics and potential future developments. It exemplifies the industry's adaptability, innovation, and significant contributions to economic growth and entrepreneurship. As we progress through the following chapters, we will delve deeper into the various facets of private equity, providing you with a comprehensive understanding of this dynamic asset class.

Understanding the Role of Private Equity in Corporate Finance

To truly grasp the significance of private equity, it's essential to recognize its pivotal role within the realm of corporate finance. Private equity is not just an investment strategy; it's a dynamic force that shapes the financial landscape in profound ways. In this section, we delve into the multifaceted role of private equity in corporate finance, shedding light on its influence, strategies, and contributions.

Strategic Capital Infusion: Private equity serves as a strategic source of capital for companies at various stages of their lifecycle. Whether it's nurturing startups with venture capital or providing growth capital to expanding businesses, private equity firms infuse much-needed funds to fuel innovation, expansion, and transformation.

Facilitating Business Expansion: Private equity plays a critical role in fostering business growth and expansion. By providing capital and expertise, private equity investors empower companies to enter new markets, develop innovative products, and pursue strategic acquisitions.

Unlocking Value through Buyouts: Leveraged buyouts (LBOs), a prominent private equity strategy, offer a path to value creation. Private equity firms acquire public or private companies, often leveraging debt, with the goal of optimizing operations, improving profitability, and generating substantial returns for investors.

Operational Excellence: A distinguishing feature of private equity is its hands-on approach. Private equity investors actively engage with portfolio companies, working collaboratively to enhance operational efficiency, streamline processes, and implement strategic initiatives. This approach goes beyond passive ownership and contributes to value creation.

Long-Term Perspective: Private equity takes a patient and long-term view of investments. Unlike the short-term focus of public markets, private equity investors are willing to commit capital for several years.

This extended investment horizon allows for comprehensive strategic planning and the pursuit of sustainable growth.

Crisis Management: In times of economic downturns or financial distress, private equity often steps in as a stabilizing force. Distressed asset acquisition is a strategic maneuver wherein private equity firms acquire distressed companies, revitalize operations, and position them for future success.

Exit Strategies: Private equity's role extends to the orchestration of exit strategies. Whether through initial public offerings (IPOs), secondary sales, or strategic acquisitions, private equity firms meticulously plan and execute exits to realize returns and generate liquidity for investors.

Innovative Financing Structures: Private equity is known for its creativity in financing structures. Mezzanine financing, for instance, combines elements of debt and equity to fund growth initiatives. These innovative structures offer flexibility and tailored solutions to meet specific financing needs.

Contributions to Economic Growth: Private equity's contributions to economic growth are substantial. It fosters entrepreneurship, job creation, and innovation. By supporting promising companies and providing the resources needed for expansion, private equity firms contribute to economic dynamism.

Global Reach: Private equity transcends geographical boundaries. It engages in cross-border investments, facilitating international business expansion and fostering global economic interconnectedness.

Risk Management: Private equity firms carefully assess and manage risks associated with their investments. This disciplined approach to risk management contributes to the stability and sustainability of portfolio companies.

Understanding the multifaceted role of private equity in corporate finance is essential for comprehending its far-reaching impact on businesses, economies, and financial markets. As we journey through subsequent chapters, we will delve deeper into the intricacies of private equity, exploring its various strategies, valuation methods, and the evolving landscape of this dynamic asset class.

Key Players in the Private Equity Industry

As we navigate the landscape of private equity, it becomes evident that this industry is characterized by a diverse cast of key players. These individuals and entities contribute to the dynamism and evolution of private equity. In this section, we shed light on the central figures and organizations that shape the private equity landscape.

Private Equity Firms: Private equity firms are the core entities involved in managing private equity funds. These firms raise capital from investors, such as pension funds, endowments, and high-net-worth individuals, and deploy it into a portfolio of private companies. They are responsible for sourcing investment opportunities, conducting due diligence, executing transactions, and actively managing portfolio companies.

Limited Partners (LPs): Limited partners are the investors in private equity funds. These may include institutional investors like pension funds, insurance companies, and university endowments, as well as individual investors. LPs commit capital to private equity funds with the expectation of earning a return on their investment.

General Partners (GPs): General partners are the professionals within private equity firms responsible for managing the funds and making investment decisions. GPs have fiduciary duties to the limited partners and are typically compensated through a combination of management fees and a share of the fund's profits, known as carried interest.

Portfolio Company Executives: Executives and management teams of portfolio companies play a crucial role in the private equity ecosystem. They collaborate with private equity investors to implement growth strategies, operational improvements, and other initiatives aimed at creating value within the portfolio companies.

Advisory Firms: Advisory firms, including investment banks and consulting firms, often provide specialized services to both private equity firms and portfolio companies. These services may include financial advisory, due diligence, valuation, and strategic consulting.

Law Firms: Legal experts and law firms play a pivotal role in private equity transactions. They assist in structuring deals, drafting legal documents, ensuring regulatory compliance, and navigating complex legal issues.

Accounting Firms: Accounting firms offer financial expertise and audit services to private equity firms and portfolio companies. They assist in financial reporting, tax planning, and ensuring compliance with accounting standards.

Placement Agents: Placement agents are intermediaries that help private equity firms raise capital from investors. They play a critical role in fund marketing, investor relations, and facilitating connections between GPs and potential LPs.

Fund of Funds: Fund of funds are investment vehicles that pool capital from multiple investors and allocate it to a diversified portfolio of private equity funds. They provide LPs with a way to gain exposure to multiple private equity strategies and managers through a single investment.

Regulatory Bodies: Regulatory authorities in various jurisdictions oversee private equity activities to ensure compliance with securities laws and protect the interests of investors. These bodies may impose reporting requirements, registration obligations, and other regulatory measures.

Entrepreneurs and Founders: Entrepreneurs and founders of companies seeking capital for growth or succession planning are essential participants in the private equity ecosystem. Private equity firms provide a source of funding and expertise to support their entrepreneurial visions.

Investment Professionals: Professionals in the private equity industry, including analysts, associates, and partners, contribute their expertise in deal sourcing, due diligence, financial analysis, and portfolio management.

Understanding the roles and interactions of these key players is essential for comprehending the intricacies of private equity investments and transactions. Throughout the book, we will delve deeper into the strategies, practices, and evolving dynamics that define the private equity industry.

Chapter 2: Types of Private Equity Investments

Venture Capital vs. Buyout/Private Equity

Within the realm of private equity investments, there exists a diverse array of strategies, each tailored to specific stages of a company's lifecycle and investment objectives. Two prominent categories within this spectrum are venture capital and buyout/private equity. In this section, we explore the distinctions and dynamics that set these investment approaches apart.

Venture Capital (VC):

- **Stage Focus**: Venture capital primarily targets early-stage and startup companies. These companies often have innovative ideas, products, or technologies but may not yet have established revenue streams or profitability.

- **Capital Injection**: VC firms provide capital to fuel the growth and development of startups. This capital is typically used for product development, market expansion, and scaling operations.

- **Risk Profile**: Venture capital investments are inherently high-risk due to the early-stage nature of the companies involved. These investments are characterized by a higher probability of failure but offer the potential for substantial returns if successful.

- **Active Involvement**: VC investors often take an active role in mentoring and guiding the entrepreneurs behind the startups. They provide valuable expertise and networking opportunities to help startups navigate challenges and accelerate growth.

◈ **Exit Strategies**: Common exit strategies for venture capital investments include initial public offerings (IPOs), acquisitions by larger companies, or secondary sales to other investors. The goal is to realize significant returns on successful investments.

Buyout/Private Equity:

◈ **Stage Focus**: Buyout and private equity investments typically target more mature companies. These companies may already have established revenue streams, market presence, and operational histories.

◈ **Capital Injection**: Private equity firms acquire established companies, often using a combination of equity and debt financing. The goal is to optimize operations, drive efficiency, and enhance profitability.

◈ **Risk Profile**: While private equity investments carry risks, they are generally perceived as having a more moderate risk profile compared to venture capital. The focus on established companies with a track record can mitigate some of the uncertainties associated with startups.

◈ **Operational Improvement**: Private equity investors actively engage with portfolio companies to implement operational improvements, cost efficiencies, and strategic initiatives. This hands-on approach is central to the private equity strategy.

◈ **Exit Strategies**: Exit strategies for private equity investments include selling portfolio companies to other investors, conducting secondary sales, or taking companies public through IPOs. The objective is to realize returns and generate liquidity for investors.

Overlap and Diversity:

It's important to note that the private equity landscape is not rigidly defined, and there can be overlap between venture capital and buyout/ private equity. Some private equity firms may engage in both venture capital and buyout investments, depending on their investment mandates and strategies.

Hybrid Strategies:

In addition to venture capital and buyout strategies, there are hybrid approaches that bridge the gap between these two categories. For example, growth equity focuses on investing in companies that have passed the startup phase but still have significant growth potential.

Diverse Investment Opportunities:

The diversity of private equity strategies allows investors to tailor their portfolios to their risk tolerance and investment objectives. Whether seeking high-risk, high-reward opportunities in startups or pursuing more established companies with growth potential, private equity offers a spectrum of investment choices.

Understanding the distinctions between venture capital and buyout/ private equity is crucial for investors and entrepreneurs alike. These strategies serve different stages of the corporate lifecycle and come with unique risk-return profiles, making them valuable tools for capital allocation and growth. In subsequent chapters, we will delve deeper into various private equity strategies and their applications.

Growth Equity and Mezzanine Financing

In addition to venture capital and buyout/private equity, the landscape of private equity investments encompasses other strategies that cater to specific investment objectives and stages of a company's development. Two such strategies are growth equity and mezzanine financing. In this section, we explore these strategies, shedding light on their characteristics and roles within the private equity spectrum.

Growth Equity:

◈ **Focus on Growth-Stage Companies**: Growth equity, sometimes referred to as growth capital, targets companies that have progressed beyond the startup phase and have established a track record of revenue generation and market presence. These companies are typically in the growth or expansion stage of their development.

◈ **Capital Infusion for Scaling**: Growth equity firms provide capital to fuel the further expansion and scaling of these established companies. The capital is deployed to support initiatives such as market expansion, product development, and strategic acquisitions.

◈ **Moderate to Lower Risk Profile**: Growth equity investments generally carry a moderate risk profile compared to venture capital. Since the focus is on more mature companies with proven business models, the uncertainty associated with startups is reduced.

◈ **Minority or Majority Ownership**: Growth equity investors may acquire minority or majority ownership stakes in portfolio companies, depending on the specific deal structure and objectives. In some cases, they partner with existing management teams to drive growth.

⟐ **Alignment with Long-Term Growth**: The primary goal of growth equity is to align the interests of investors and management in achieving long-term growth and value creation. Investors often take a collaborative approach, working alongside company leadership to achieve strategic objectives.

⟐ **Exit Strategies**: Common exit strategies for growth equity investments include secondary sales, selling to other investors or private equity firms, or potentially taking the company public through an IPO. The objective is to realize returns and provide liquidity to investors.

Mezzanine Financing:

⟐ **Hybrid Debt-Equity Financing**: Mezzanine financing represents a hybrid form of financing that combines elements of debt and equity. It often takes the form of subordinated debt or preferred equity. Mezzanine lenders provide capital to companies in need of additional funding for various purposes.

⟐ **Risk and Return**: Mezzanine financing carries a higher level of risk compared to traditional bank loans but offers the potential for higher returns. Lenders accept a subordinate position in the capital structure, which means they have a lower priority in case of bankruptcy but may receive a higher interest rate or equity participation in return.

◈ **Use Cases**: Mezzanine financing is commonly used to support growth initiatives, acquisitions, management buyouts, or recapitalizations. It can serve as a flexible financing solution when companies need capital beyond what traditional lenders can offer.

◈ **Alignment with Growth**: Mezzanine lenders are often aligned with a company's growth and success. Their investment terms may include equity warrants or options, allowing them to participate in the company's upside potential.

◈ **Exit Strategies**: Mezzanine investors typically aim to exit their investments through a combination of interest payments, principal repayment, and potential equity participation. They may exit when the company refinances or is sold.

Diverse Investment Opportunities:

Growth equity and mezzanine financing represent two distinct but valuable strategies within the private equity landscape. While growth equity focuses on supporting the growth of established companies, mezzanine financing provides flexible capital solutions that can accommodate a range of financing needs.

Investors and entrepreneurs alike can benefit from understanding these strategies and how they can be tailored to specific business objectives and growth stages. In the chapters ahead, we will continue to explore various private equity strategies and their applications in greater detail.

Distressed and Special Situations Investing

Within the realm of private equity investments, there exist specialized strategies designed to seize unique opportunities presented by distressed companies and special situations. In this section, we delve into the strategies of distressed investing and special situations investing, shedding light on their characteristics and roles within the private equity landscape.

Distressed Investing:

- **Focus on Troubled Companies:** Distressed investing, as the name suggests, revolves around troubled or financially distressed companies. These companies may be facing financial distress, operational challenges, or the threat of insolvency.

- **Capital Infusion and Turnaround:** Distressed investors, often private equity firms with expertise in distressed situations, provide capital to troubled companies with the aim of facilitating a turnaround. The capital is typically used to address immediate liquidity needs, restructure operations, and stabilize the company.

- **Risk and Opportunity:** Distressed investing is characterized by a higher level of risk due to the challenges faced by distressed companies. However, it presents the opportunity for substantial returns if the turnaround is successful and value is unlocked.

- **Active Restructuring:** Distressed investors play an active role in the restructuring process. They may take control of the distressed company, implement cost-cutting measures, negotiate with creditors, and make strategic decisions to improve the company's financial health.

- **Exit Strategies**: Exit strategies for distressed investments can vary. Successful turnarounds may result in the sale of the revitalized company or an IPO. In some cases, the company may be sold in parts or merged with other entities.

Special Situations Investing:

- **Versatility in Approach**: Special situations investing encompasses a wide range of opportunities beyond distressed situations. It includes investments in companies facing unique circumstances, such as mergers, acquisitions, divestitures, restructurings, or regulatory changes.

- **Adaptability**: Special situations investors are known for their adaptability and ability to tailor their strategies to specific opportunities. They leverage their financial acumen and creativity to navigate complex situations and unlock value.

- **Risk and Reward**: Special situations can carry varying degrees of risk and reward, depending on the nature of the opportunity. Some situations may involve regulatory uncertainties, while others may offer arbitrage opportunities or the potential for rapid value creation.

- **Active Involvement**: In special situations, investors often play an active role in navigating the unique circumstances. They may engage in negotiations, legal proceedings, or strategic actions to maximize returns.

- **Exit Strategies**: Exit strategies for special situations investments are diverse and depend on the specific circumstances. Investors may seek to capitalize on short-term market opportunities or position themselves for long-term value creation.

Diverse Investment Opportunities:

Distressed and special situations investing represent niche but strategically significant segments of the private equity landscape. While distressed investing focuses on rescuing troubled companies, special situations investing capitalizes on unique opportunities that require creative solutions.

Understanding these specialized strategies is essential for investors seeking to explore alternative avenues within private equity. These strategies allow investors to target opportunities that may be overlooked by traditional investment approaches. In the upcoming chapters, we will continue to explore various private equity strategies and their applications in greater detail.

Secondary Market Transactions

Within the diverse universe of private equity investments, secondary market transactions represent a distinct approach that offers unique advantages and opportunities. In this section, we delve into secondary market transactions, shedding light on their characteristics and the role they play within the private equity landscape.

Secondary Market Transactions:

- **Nature of Transactions**: Secondary market transactions involve the buying and selling of existing private equity fund investments. These investments are typically in the form of limited partnership interests in private equity funds.

- **Motivations**: Sellers in secondary market transactions may include institutional investors, such as pension funds, endowments, and fund-of-funds, as well as individual investors. Their motivations for selling can vary and may include portfolio rebalancing, liquidity needs, or a desire to exit specific fund investments.

◈ **Buyer Profiles**: Buyers in secondary market transactions can be diverse and include other institutional investors, private equity firms, or dedicated secondary market investment firms. These buyers seek to acquire existing fund interests as part of their investment strategy.

◈ **Benefits for Sellers**: Secondary market transactions provide sellers with liquidity and the ability to exit their investments before the fund's natural term expires. This can be especially valuable for institutional investors with specific liquidity requirements.

◈ **Benefits for Buyers**: Buyers in secondary transactions gain access to established private equity fund portfolios without having to commit to the fund's full term. They may see opportunities for value creation or diversification within the acquired portfolio.

◈ **Price Negotiation**: The pricing of secondary market transactions can be negotiated between buyers and sellers. The price may reflect various factors, including the net asset value (NAV) of the fund, the perceived future value of the fund's assets, and the terms of the transaction.

◈ **Due Diligence**: Both buyers and sellers typically conduct due diligence to assess the underlying assets in the fund portfolio. This due diligence includes evaluating the financial health and potential of the portfolio companies.

- **Impact on Fund Operations**: Secondary market transactions do not directly impact the operations of the underlying portfolio companies. The fund's management remains responsible for overseeing the portfolio and implementing the fund's investment strategy.

- **Market Dynamics**: The secondary market for private equity fund interests has grown in size and sophistication over the years. It has become an integral part of the private equity ecosystem, providing liquidity and flexibility to investors.

Diverse Investment Opportunities:

Secondary market transactions offer investors a unique way to access and manage their exposure to private equity. Sellers can achieve liquidity, while buyers can acquire diverse portfolios of private equity fund interests. This flexibility allows investors to tailor their private equity holdings to their specific needs and objectives.

Understanding the dynamics of secondary market transactions is essential for both buyers and sellers in the private equity space. It is a strategic tool that allows investors to navigate the evolving landscape of private equity investments. In the upcoming chapters, we will continue to explore various private equity strategies and their applications in greater detail.

Chapter 3: Fundraising and Fund Structures

Fundraising Process in Private Equity

In the world of private equity, the process of raising capital is a fundamental and intricate aspect of the industry's operations. Successful fundraising is essential for private equity firms to assemble the financial resources needed to execute their investment strategies effectively. In this section, we delve into the nuanced and strategic process of fundraising in private equity.

Building Investor Relationships:

Fundraising in private equity begins with the cultivation and maintenance of relationships with potential investors. These investors, often referred to as Limited Partners (LPs), include institutional entities such as pension funds, endowments, foundations, family offices, high-net-worth individuals, and fund-of-funds. Establishing trust and credibility is paramount during this phase.

Fund Strategy and Offering:

Private equity firms must articulate a clear and compelling investment strategy that aligns with the interests and objectives of potential investors. This strategy defines the types of investments the fund will pursue, such as venture capital, buyouts, distressed assets, or special situations. It also outlines the fund's geographic focus, industry preferences, and risk-return profile.

Fund Documents and Legal Structure:

Fundraising involves the preparation of comprehensive legal documents, including the Private Placement Memorandum (PPM) and the Limited Partnership Agreement (LPA). These documents outline the terms, conditions, and expectations of the fund and its investors. Private equity funds typically take the form of Limited Partnerships (LPs) or Limited Liability Companies (LLCs).

Fund Marketing and Roadshows:

Private equity firms engage in marketing efforts to promote their fund's merits and investment opportunities. This may involve conducting roadshows, where firm representatives meet with potential investors to present the fund's strategy, track record, and competitive advantages. Effective marketing is crucial for attracting investor commitments.

Due Diligence and Selection:

Investors conduct thorough due diligence on private equity firms and their funds before making commitments. This due diligence process involves evaluating the firm's track record, investment team, risk management practices, and alignment of interests. Conversely, private equity firms assess potential investors to ensure they align with the fund's strategy and objectives.

Fundraising Target and Commitments:

Private equity firms establish fundraising targets, indicating the amount of capital they aim to raise for the fund. Investors commit capital to the fund based on their level of interest and alignment with the fund's strategy. Fundraising efforts continue until the target is met or until a predetermined closing date.

First Close and Interim Investments:

Once a sufficient amount of capital is raised, private equity funds may conduct a "first close." This initial closing allows the fund to commence investments while fundraising efforts continue. Interim investments may be made in line with the fund's strategy.

Subsequent Closes and Capital Calls:

Private equity funds often conduct subsequent closings as additional commitments are secured. Capital calls are made to investors when opportunities for investment arise. These calls require investors to fulfill their financial commitments to the fund.

Transparency and Reporting:

Private equity firms maintain transparency by providing regular reporting to investors. This includes financial statements, performance updates, and details on portfolio investments. Maintaining open communication with investors is essential for building trust.

Fundraising Challenges:

The fundraising process in private equity is not without its challenges. Competition for investor capital is fierce, and market conditions can impact the fundraising environment. Successfully navigating these challenges requires a compelling investment thesis, a strong track record, and effective relationship management.

Understanding the intricacies of the fundraising process is vital for private equity professionals, investors, and anyone interested in participating in this dynamic asset class. In the chapters ahead, we will continue to explore the various facets of private equity, including fund structures, investment strategies, and the evolving landscape of this industry.

Types of Private Equity Funds

Within the realm of private equity, a diverse array of fund structures exists, each tailored to specific investment objectives, asset classes, and strategies. In this section, we explore the various types of private equity funds, shedding light on their characteristics and roles within the private equity landscape.

Venture Capital Funds:

- **Focus on Early-Stage Companies**: Venture capital funds specialize in financing early-stage and startup companies with high growth potential. These companies often operate in technology, biotechnology, and innovative sectors.

- **Investment Objective**: Venture capital funds aim to provide capital to support product development, market expansion, and growth initiatives in exchange for equity ownership. The goal is to participate in the success of emerging companies.

- **Risk and Reward**: Venture capital investments are characterized by a higher level of risk due to the early-stage nature of the companies. However, they offer the potential for significant returns if the portfolio includes successful startups.

Buyout Funds:

- **Focus on Established Companies**: Buyout funds, also known as private equity buyout funds, target established and mature companies. These companies may have established revenue streams, market presence, and operational histories.

- **Investment Objective**: Buyout funds acquire controlling or significant ownership stakes in target companies with the goal of optimizing operations, driving efficiency, and enhancing profitability. The focus is on value creation through operational improvements.

◈ **Risk and Reward**: Buyout investments generally carry a more moderate risk profile compared to venture capital. The emphasis on established companies with a track record helps mitigate some of the uncertainties associated with startups.

Real Estate Private Equity Funds:

◈ **Focus on Real Estate Assets**: Real estate private equity funds invest in a variety of real estate assets, including residential, commercial, industrial, and hospitality properties. Their objective is to generate returns through property acquisitions, development, or repositioning.

◈ **Investment Objective**: Real estate private equity funds aim to create value through active management of real estate assets. This may involve renovating properties, optimizing leasing, or pursuing development projects.

◈ **Risk and Reward**: Real estate private equity investments can vary in risk depending on the specific strategy and asset class. These investments offer the potential for income generation, capital appreciation, and diversification.

Infrastructure Funds:

◈ **Focus on Infrastructure Assets**: Infrastructure funds target investments in essential infrastructure assets, such as transportation, energy, utilities, and telecommunications. These assets often have long-term revenue streams and serve as critical components of society.

◈ **Investment Objective**: Infrastructure funds seek stable, long-term cash flows from their investments. They may involve public-private partnerships (PPPs) and focus on infrastructure development, operation, and maintenance.

◈ **Risk and Reward**: Infrastructure investments are generally considered lower risk due to the essential nature of the assets. They provide income-generating opportunities with a focus on long-term stability.

Private Debt Funds:

◈ **Focus on Debt Instruments**: Private debt funds invest in debt securities and loans issued by companies. They provide debt financing to companies for various purposes, including growth, acquisitions, and refinancing.

◈ **Investment Objective**: Private debt funds aim to generate returns through interest income and capital preservation. They offer an alternative source of financing for companies outside the traditional banking sector.

◈ **Risk and Reward**: Private debt investments offer the potential for steady income with a risk profile typically lower than that of equity investments. The risk varies depending on the credit quality of the underlying borrowers.

These are just a few examples of the diverse types of private equity funds that investors can access. Each fund type has its own risk-return profile and investment strategy, allowing investors to diversify their portfolios and tailor their exposure to specific asset classes and sectors.

Understanding the nuances of these fund types is crucial for investors seeking to navigate the private equity landscape effectively. In the chapters ahead, we will continue to explore various private equity fund structures and strategies, offering a comprehensive understanding of this dynamic asset class.

Fund Structure and Limited Partnerships

Private equity funds are typically structured as limited partnerships, a legal framework that plays a central role in defining the relationships and responsibilities among various stakeholders. In this section, we delve into the structure of private equity funds and the concept of limited partnerships, illuminating their significance within the private equity industry.

Fund Structure:

- **General Partner (GP)**: The general partner is the entity responsible for managing the private equity fund. GPs are typically private equity firms or investment professionals with expertise in fund management. They make investment decisions, execute strategies, and oversee the day-to-day operations of the fund.

- **Limited Partners (LPs)**: Limited partners are the investors in the fund. They provide capital to the fund but do not have a direct role in its management. LPs include institutional investors, high-net-worth individuals, and entities seeking exposure to private equity.

- **Management Fees**: GPs receive management fees from the fund, which cover the costs of fund administration, due diligence, and management. These fees are typically calculated as a percentage of the fund's assets under management (AUM).

◈ **Carried Interest (Carry)**: GPs are also entitled to carried interest, often referred to as "carry." Carry represents a share of the fund's profits earned from successful investments. It aligns the interests of GPs with those of LPs, as GPs receive a portion of the investment gains.

Limited Partnerships (LPs):

◈ **Limited Liability**: LPs enjoy limited liability, meaning their liability is typically limited to the amount of their capital commitments to the fund. This shields them from personal liability for the fund's obligations or losses.

◈ **Passive Investment Role**: LPs participate in the fund as passive investors, entrusting the GP with the responsibility of managing the fund's assets and investments. They do not participate in the fund's decision-making or day-to-day operations.

◈ **Capital Commitments**: LPs commit to providing a specified amount of capital to the fund over a predetermined timeframe. These capital commitments are drawn upon by the GP as needed for investments and expenses.

◈ **Income and Taxation**: LPs receive income from the fund in the form of distributions, which can include returns on investments, interest, and dividends. The tax treatment of these distributions can vary by jurisdiction and the LP's tax status.

Alignment of Interests:

The limited partnership structure fosters alignment of interests among stakeholders. GPs have a vested interest in maximizing returns for LPs, as they earn carried interest based on the fund's success. This alignment encourages GPs to make prudent investment decisions and strive for positive outcomes.

Fund Governance and Agreements:

The governance and operation of private equity funds are governed by legal agreements, primarily the Limited Partnership Agreement (LPA). LPAs define the terms, conditions, and responsibilities of both GPs and LPs, including matters related to capital commitments, fees, carry, decision-making, and exit strategies.

Capital Calls and Distributions:

Private equity funds employ a "capital call" mechanism, which allows GPs to request capital from LPs as needed for investments and expenses. Conversely, "distributions" involve the return of capital and profits to LPs when investments are monetized or generate returns.

Transparency and Reporting:

GPs are typically required to provide regular reporting to LPs, including financial statements, performance updates, and details on fund investments. Maintaining transparency and open communication is essential for building trust between GPs and LPs.

Understanding the structure of private equity funds and the role of limited partnerships is essential for investors and professionals in the private equity industry. This structure not only defines the legal framework but also shapes the relationships and incentives that drive the success of private equity investments. In the chapters ahead, we will continue to explore various aspects of private equity, including investment strategies, risk management, and industry trends.

Investor Due Diligence in Fundraising

In the intricate world of private equity fundraising, due diligence plays a pivotal role in shaping successful investment partnerships. For both General Partners (GPs) and Limited Partners (LPs), the due diligence process is a comprehensive evaluation of the fund's strategy, management team, and alignment of interests. In this section, we delve into the critical aspects of investor due diligence in the context of private equity fundraising.

Investor's Perspective:

For LPs, the due diligence process serves as a mechanism to evaluate the merits and risks associated with a private equity fund. It's a critical step in the decision-making process before committing capital to a fund. Key considerations during due diligence include:

1. **Fund Strategy and Investment Thesis**: LPs assess the fund's investment strategy, including its focus on asset classes, sectors, geographic regions, and risk-return profile. They seek alignment between the fund's strategy and their own investment objectives.

2. **Track Record and Performance**: LPs examine the GP's historical track record and performance. This involves scrutinizing the GP's previous funds, investment outcomes, and the ability to deliver returns consistent with the fund's strategy.

3. **Investment Team**: LPs evaluate the composition and experience of the GP's investment team. They assess whether the team possesses the necessary expertise, industry knowledge, and operational capabilities to execute the fund's strategy effectively.

4. Alignment of Interests: Ensuring that the GP's interests align with those of LPs is a fundamental aspect of due diligence. LPs scrutinize the fee structure, carried interest arrangements, and co-investment opportunities to assess alignment.

5. Risk Management: LPs inquire about the fund's risk management practices, including strategies for mitigating investment risks and potential challenges. They want to understand how the fund addresses risk factors.

6. Legal and Regulatory Compliance: LPs assess the fund's legal and regulatory compliance, including adherence to relevant securities laws and industry standards. This ensures that the fund operates within legal boundaries.

7. Fund Terms and Conditions: LPs carefully review the terms and conditions outlined in the Limited Partnership Agreement (LPA) and the Private Placement Memorandum (PPM). This includes commitments, fees, distribution policies, and exit strategies.

8. Fundraising Process: LPs may inquire about the fund's fundraising process, the timeline for capital commitments, and the mechanics of capital calls and distributions.

GP's Perspective:

On the flip side, GPs also conduct due diligence on potential LPs to ensure they align with the fund's strategy and objectives. This process includes:

1. Assessing Alignment: GPs evaluate whether the LP's investment goals and expectations align with the fund's strategy. They seek LPs who complement the fund's objectives.

2. Financial Suitability: GPs assess the financial suitability of potential LPs, ensuring they have the capacity to meet their capital commitments and participate effectively in the fund.

3. Regulatory Compliance: GPs verify that LPs comply with legal and regulatory requirements, as violations could impact the fund's operations.

4. Reputation and Stability: GPs consider the reputation, stability, and reliability of potential LPs, as their involvement can influence the fund's dynamics.

5. Contribution Beyond Capital: GPs may also assess whether LPs bring additional value beyond capital, such as industry expertise, network connections, or strategic insights.

Mutual Trust and Transparency:

A successful private equity fundraising process hinges on mutual trust, transparency, and alignment of interests between GPs and LPs. Effective due diligence allows both parties to make informed decisions and establish a solid foundation for a long-term investment partnership.

In the chapters ahead, we will continue to explore various facets of private equity, including fund structures, investment strategies, and the evolving landscape of this dynamic asset class.

Chapter 4: Private Equity Investment Strategies

Investment Strategy Framework

Private equity investment strategies are diverse and dynamic, shaped by a fund's objectives, risk appetite, and market conditions. In this section, we establish a framework for understanding private equity investment strategies, highlighting the key elements that guide decision-making and portfolio construction.

1. Investment Objectives:

a. Capital Appreciation: Many private equity funds seek capital appreciation by investing in companies with the potential for substantial growth. The primary goal is to increase the value of portfolio companies over the investment horizon.

b. Income Generation: Some private equity strategies focus on income generation through investments in established companies with stable cash flows. These strategies prioritize regular distributions to investors.

c. Risk Mitigation: Certain private equity strategies emphasize risk mitigation by targeting assets or sectors with defensive characteristics. Preservation of capital and stable returns are paramount in these strategies.

2. Investment Horizon:

a. Short-Term: Short-term strategies typically involve investments with a horizon of a few years. These strategies may include distressed investing, opportunistic acquisitions, or special situations that offer quick value realization.

b. Medium-Term: Medium-term strategies encompass investments with a horizon of several years. Buyout and growth equity strategies often fall into this category, allowing time for operational improvements and value creation.

c. Long-Term: Long-term strategies involve investments with extended horizons, often spanning a decade or more. Infrastructure, real estate, and certain venture capital strategies may have longer investment horizons.

3. Risk-Reward Profile:

a. High Risk-High Reward: Some strategies embrace higher risk for the potential of significant returns. Venture capital, early-stage investments, and distressed asset acquisitions are examples of high-risk, high-reward strategies.

b. Moderate Risk-Moderate Reward: Buyout and growth equity strategies typically fall into this category, balancing risk and reward by focusing on established companies with growth potential.

c. Low Risk-Low Reward: Defensive strategies, such as income-focused investments in stable sectors, prioritize lower-risk profiles and more predictable returns.

4. Asset Class and Sector Focus:

a. Equity Investments: Private equity funds primarily invest in equity securities, acquiring ownership stakes in portfolio companies. These investments offer the potential for capital appreciation.

b. Real Assets: Some strategies focus on real assets such as real estate, infrastructure, or natural resources. These assets often provide income generation and stability.

c. **Debt and Credit**: Private debt strategies involve lending capital to companies through various debt instruments, offering predictable income and capital preservation.

5. **Geographic Focus**:

a. **Domestic**: Funds may concentrate on investments within a specific country or region, allowing for in-depth knowledge of local markets and regulations.

b. **International**: Global or international strategies expand the investment universe, offering diversification and exposure to a broader range of opportunities.

6. **Specialization**:

a. **Sector Specialization**: Some funds specialize in specific industry sectors, leveraging industry expertise to identify and capitalize on opportunities within their chosen field.

b. **Niche Strategies**: Niche strategies target specialized markets, asset classes, or investment themes, such as healthcare, technology, or sustainable investments.

7. **Value Creation Approach**:

a. **Operational Enhancement**: Strategies may focus on operational improvements within portfolio companies, implementing changes to boost efficiency, reduce costs, and enhance profitability.

b. **Financial Engineering**: Certain strategies employ financial engineering techniques, such as leveraging balance sheets or optimizing capital structures, to create value.

c. Market Timing: Opportunistic strategies involve identifying and seizing market timing opportunities, such as distressed investing during economic downturns.

8. Exit Strategies:

a. Trade Sale: Many private equity investments culminate in trade sales, where portfolio companies are sold to strategic buyers within the same industry.

b. IPOs: Initial Public Offerings (IPOs) provide exit opportunities, allowing portfolio companies to go public and list their shares on stock exchanges.

c. Secondary Sales: In some cases, secondary sales to other private equity firms or investors may offer exit options.

9. Risk Management:

a. Risk Mitigation: Strategies may include risk mitigation measures, such as diversification, hedging, or downside protection mechanisms.

b. Portfolio Monitoring: Rigorous monitoring of portfolio companies and active management are crucial elements of risk management.

10. Alignment with LP Objectives:

Ultimately, private equity investment strategies must align with the objectives and risk tolerance of Limited Partners (LPs). The selection of a specific strategy reflects the LP's desired exposure to private equity and the fund's ability to deliver on those objectives.

This framework provides a foundation for understanding the various dimensions of private equity investment strategies. In the subsequent chapters, we will delve deeper into specific strategies, their implementation, and the factors influencing success in the private equity landscape.

Value Creation in Private Equity

Private equity, as an asset class, is synonymous with its central tenet: value creation. Within this investment realm, value creation represents the core objective, where General Partners (GPs) aim to enhance the worth of portfolio companies over time. In this section, we explore the multifaceted strategies employed in private equity to achieve this pivotal goal.

Operational Enhancement:

Operational enhancement is a cornerstone of value creation in private equity. It involves optimizing the operational aspects of portfolio companies to drive efficiency, reduce costs, and enhance profitability. Key strategies include:

1. Cost Rationalization: GPs scrutinize the cost structure of portfolio companies, identifying inefficiencies and redundancies. They implement measures to reduce operational costs while maintaining or improving service quality.

2. Revenue Growth: Driving top-line growth is equally critical. GPs work with management teams to identify revenue-enhancing opportunities, such as expanding market share, launching new products or services, or entering new geographic markets.

3. Talent Management: Attracting and retaining top talent is paramount. GPs support portfolio companies in talent acquisition, leadership development, and organizational structure improvements to foster a high-performance culture.

Financial Engineering:

Financial engineering involves leveraging financial strategies and instruments to create value. This approach includes optimizing capital structures, improving working capital management, and utilizing debt instruments effectively. Key elements include:

1. **Debt Optimization**: GPs assess the capital structure of portfolio companies, considering the optimal mix of equity and debt. They may refinance or recapitalize to reduce borrowing costs or release capital for growth initiatives.

2. **Working Capital Management**: Efficient management of working capital, including receivables, payables, and inventory, can release cash that can be reinvested or used to reduce debt.

3. **Leveraged Buyouts**: In buyout strategies, GPs employ leverage to acquire companies. The judicious use of debt can amplify returns when combined with operational improvements.

Market Timing and Strategic Initiatives:

Strategic timing plays a crucial role in value creation. GPs may opportunistically time investments, such as acquiring distressed assets during economic downturns. Additionally, strategic initiatives can include:

1. **Mergers and Acquisitions (M&A)**: M&A activities, either consolidating existing portfolio companies or acquiring complementary businesses, can create synergies and enhance competitiveness.

2. **Market Expansion**: Expanding into new markets or geographic regions can drive growth. This strategy may involve organic expansion, joint ventures, or strategic partnerships.

Alignment of Interests:

Ensuring alignment of interests between GPs and Limited Partners (LPs) is integral to value creation. GPs earn carried interest, or "carry," based on the fund's performance, fostering alignment. This shared success incentive ensures GPs are motivated to maximize returns.

Exit Strategies:

Realizing value is contingent on the choice of exit strategies. GPs employ various exit options, including:

1. **Trade Sale**: Selling portfolio companies to strategic buyers within the same industry often realizes substantial value.

2. **Initial Public Offerings (IPOs)**: Taking portfolio companies public through IPOs can unlock value through stock market listings.

3. **Secondary Sales**: Selling portfolio companies to other private equity firms or investors provides exit opportunities.

Portfolio Monitoring and Active Management:

Rigorous portfolio monitoring and active management are essential elements of value creation. GPs continuously assess the performance of portfolio companies, adjust strategies as needed, and make timely decisions to optimize outcomes.

Risk Mitigation:

Value creation strategies encompass risk mitigation measures. GPs employ diversification, hedging, and downside protection mechanisms to safeguard investments and mitigate potential losses.

In essence, value creation in private equity is a dynamic and multifaceted endeavor. GPs draw upon their expertise in operational improvement, financial engineering, strategic vision, and prudent risk management to maximize returns for their investors. In the chapters ahead, we will explore specific private equity investment strategies, their nuances, and their roles within the broader private equity landscape.

Active Ownership and Operational Improvements

In the realm of private equity, active ownership and operational improvements are not just strategies; they are guiding principles that underpin the core of value creation. Private equity firms, as stewards of portfolio companies, take an active role in enhancing the operational and strategic aspects of their investments. In this section, we delve into the significance of active ownership and the methodologies used to effect operational improvements.

Active Ownership: A Hands-On Approach:

Active ownership signifies more than just a passive investment. It involves proactive engagement, collaboration, and influence over portfolio companies. Key facets of active ownership include:

1. **Strategic Direction**: Private equity firms work closely with the management teams of portfolio companies to chart strategic direction. This may involve setting clear objectives, defining growth strategies, and aligning resources accordingly.

2. **Governance**: Active ownership often leads to governance enhancements. Private equity firms may appoint representatives to the board of directors, influence board composition, and participate in key governance decisions.

3. **Talent Management**: Attracting and retaining top talent is vital for operational excellence. Active owners assist portfolio companies in recruiting, leadership development, and performance evaluation.

4. Value Creation Roadmap: Active ownership includes the development and execution of a value creation roadmap. This strategic plan outlines the steps, milestones, and initiatives required to enhance the company's value over time.

Operational Improvements: The Engine of Value Creation:

Operational improvements are the engine that drives value creation in private equity. These improvements span various dimensions, including:

1. Cost Optimization: Private equity firms scrutinize operational costs, identifying areas for optimization and efficiency gains. Measures may include streamlining processes, renegotiating contracts, and eliminating waste.

2. Revenue Growth: Driving top-line growth is equally critical. This involves expanding market share, launching new products or services, and tapping into untapped customer segments.

3. Supply Chain Optimization: Enhancing supply chain efficiency can lead to cost savings and improved product delivery. This may involve optimizing inventory management, reducing lead times, and mitigating supply chain risks.

4. Technology Adoption: Embracing technology is often integral to operational improvements. Investments in digitalization, automation, and data analytics can enhance productivity and competitiveness.

5. Quality Control: Maintaining product or service quality is paramount. Operational improvements may include quality control measures, process standardization, and compliance with industry standards.

6. Working Capital Management: Efficient management of working capital can free up cash for growth or debt reduction. This entails optimizing accounts receivable, accounts payable, and inventory levels.

7. **International Expansion**: For companies with global ambitions, operational improvements may include expanding into international markets. This involves navigating regulatory challenges, understanding local customer dynamics, and establishing a global footprint.

Alignment of Interests and Incentives:

Active ownership and operational improvements are underpinned by the alignment of interests and incentives between General Partners (GPs) and Limited Partners (LPs). GPs' compensation structures, including carried interest (carry), link their financial success to the creation of value for LPs.

Risk Mitigation and Monitoring:

Operational improvements include risk mitigation strategies. Private equity firms actively monitor portfolio companies, identify potential risks, and implement measures to mitigate them. Rigorous oversight and timely decision-making are essential components of risk management.

A Holistic Approach to Value Creation:

Active ownership and operational improvements are not isolated strategies but rather a holistic approach to value creation. Private equity firms, armed with industry expertise, financial acumen, and a results-oriented mindset, are well-positioned to effect meaningful changes and enhance the worth of their portfolio companies.

In the subsequent chapters, we will explore specific private equity investment strategies, including venture capital, buyouts, and specialized sectors, to provide a comprehensive understanding of the multifaceted private equity landscape.

Exit Strategies in Private Equity

In the intricate world of private equity, successful investments culminate in strategically planned exit strategies. These exit strategies not only mark the realization of value but also determine the returns for Limited Partners (LPs) and General Partners (GPs). In this section, we explore the significance of exit strategies and various approaches employed in private equity, using real-world examples to illustrate their impact.

The Importance of Exit Strategies:

Exit strategies are pivotal in private equity for several reasons:

1. **Value Realization**: The primary goal of private equity investments is to enhance the value of portfolio companies and subsequently realize that value. Exit strategies materialize this objective.

2. **LP Returns**: Successful exits are the means by which LPs receive returns on their investments. The choice of exit strategy directly impacts the magnitude of these returns.

3. **Capital Recycling**: Successful exits generate liquidity that can be reinvested in new opportunities, allowing private equity firms to continually deploy capital and compound returns.

Common Exit Strategies:

Private equity firms employ various exit strategies, each tailored to the specific characteristics of the portfolio company and market conditions. Four common exit strategies include:

1. **Initial Public Offering (IPO):**

◈ *Example*: Private equity firm Everest Capital invested in Tech Innovators, a cutting-edge software company. After several years of active ownership, including operational improvements and strategic initiatives, Tech Innovators reached a stage where it could go public. Everest Capital orchestrated an IPO, allowing Tech Innovators to list its shares on a stock exchange. This exit strategy not only provided liquidity to LPs but also allowed Everest Capital to retain a portion of its ownership for potential future gains.

2. Trade Sale:

◈ *Example*: Acme Private Equity acquired DistriTech, a distribution company, with the goal of enhancing its operational efficiency and market presence. After successful operational improvements, Acme Private Equity received an attractive acquisition offer from a larger industry player, MegaCorp. They executed a trade sale, realizing substantial value for their investment and providing LPs with strong returns.

3. Secondary Sale to Another Private Equity Firm:

◈ *Example*: Apex Capital invested in GreenTech, a renewable energy company. After several years of value creation, Apex Capital decided to exit the investment. They explored a secondary sale to another private equity firm, Summit Partners, which saw potential in GreenTech's growth prospects. This secondary sale allowed Apex Capital to exit while maintaining its commitment to value creation in the renewable energy sector.

4. Recapitalization:

◈ *Example*: TerraNova Private Equity invested in TerraTech, a manufacturing company with a solid cash flow. Instead of a complete exit, TerraNova Private Equity opted for a recapitalization strategy. They refinanced TerraTech's capital structure, allowing the company to distribute a special dividend to LPs while retaining partial ownership and ongoing participation in future growth.

Factors Influencing Exit Strategy Selection:

The choice of exit strategy depends on several factors, including:

1. **Market Conditions**: The state of the financial markets and industry-specific conditions influence the feasibility and timing of different exit strategies.

2. **Company Performance**: The performance and growth trajectory of the portfolio company play a pivotal role in determining the most suitable exit strategy.

3. **LP Objectives**: Private equity firms must consider the expectations and objectives of their LPs, aligning the chosen exit strategy with LP preferences.

4. **Industry Dynamics**: The dynamics of the industry in which the portfolio company operates can impact the selection of an exit strategy.

Chapter 5: Deal Sourcing and Due Diligence

Deal Origination and Sourcing Strategies

In the dynamic world of private equity, successful deal sourcing and origination are essential prerequisites for identifying promising investment opportunities. Private equity firms employ a diverse array of strategies to unearth potential deals and assess their viability. In this section, we delve into the significance of deal origination and the strategies used to source investments, with real-world examples illustrating their effectiveness.

The Significance of Deal Sourcing:

Deal sourcing is the lifeblood of the private equity industry. It encompasses the process of identifying, evaluating, and ultimately selecting investment opportunities. Effective deal sourcing is critical for several reasons:

1. **Access to Opportunities**: It provides private equity firms access to a broad spectrum of investment opportunities, allowing them to cherry-pick those with the most potential.

2. **Portfolio Diversification**: A robust deal sourcing strategy enables firms to diversify their portfolio across different industries, geographies, and investment stages.

3. **Competitive Edge**: Successful deal sourcing can give firms a competitive advantage by allowing them to identify and act on opportunities ahead of their competitors.

4. Value Creation: The ability to identify undervalued assets or companies with growth potential is integral to value creation in private equity.

Common Deal Sourcing Strategies:

Private equity firms employ various deal sourcing strategies, often tailored to their specific focus areas and investment criteria. Four common deal sourcing strategies include:

1. Proprietary Relationships:

> ⟐ *Example*: Vista Capital, a technology-focused private equity firm, has cultivated deep relationships with key players in the tech industry. These relationships grant them exclusive access to early-stage startups and emerging technology companies. Vista Capital leverages these proprietary relationships to source deals that are not widely available in the market.

2. Industry Specialization:

> ⟐ *Example*: Nexus Equity Partners specializes in the healthcare sector. They have a dedicated team of industry experts who constantly monitor healthcare trends, attend conferences, and engage with industry stakeholders. This specialization enables Nexus Equity Partners to identify investment opportunities in healthcare companies poised for growth.

3. Scanning Emerging Markets:

> ⟐ *Example*: Frontier Capital, known for its investments in software and tech-enabled business services, actively scans

emerging markets. They recognize that innovation often thrives in these markets, and by staying ahead of the curve, they source investments in companies with disruptive potential.

4. Proactive Outreach:

◈ *Example*: Atlas Equity Partners takes a proactive approach to deal sourcing. They maintain an extensive network of intermediaries, including investment bankers, brokers, and business advisors. Atlas Equity Partners regularly communicates their investment criteria, encouraging these intermediaries to bring potential deals to their attention.

Factors Influencing Deal Origination Strategies:

The choice of deal origination strategy depends on several factors:

1. Investment Focus: The specific sectors or industries in which a private equity firm specializes influence the most effective sourcing strategies.

2. Geographic Focus: The geographic scope of a firm's investments determines whether they source deals locally, nationally, or internationally.

3. Network and Relationships: The strength of a firm's network and relationships within the business and investment community plays a crucial role in deal origination.

4. Investment Stage: Whether a firm focuses on early-stage ventures, growth companies, or mature businesses also influences sourcing strategies.

Due Diligence Process in Private Equity

In the world of private equity, the due diligence process is a meticulous and essential step that precedes any investment. It serves as the investigative foundation upon which investment decisions are based. In this section, we delve into the significance of due diligence in private equity and the comprehensive process through which potential investments are rigorously examined.

The Significance of Due Diligence:

Due diligence is the process by which private equity firms thoroughly examine the financial, operational, legal, and strategic aspects of a potential investment. It is a critical step for several reasons:

1. **Risk Mitigation**: Due diligence helps identify and assess risks associated with the investment, enabling private equity firms to make informed decisions and develop risk mitigation strategies.

2. **Valuation**: It plays a pivotal role in determining the fair value of the target company. Accurate valuation is essential for negotiating a favorable deal and aligning investment with expected returns.

3. **Strategic Alignment**: Due diligence ensures that the target company aligns with the private equity firm's investment thesis and strategy. It verifies whether the investment fits within the firm's portfolio and long-term objectives.

4. **Legal and Regulatory Compliance**: It verifies that the target company complies with all legal and regulatory requirements, mitigating the risk of legal issues arising post-investment.

5. **Operational Assessment**: Due diligence assesses the operational efficiency of the target company. This examination identifies opportunities for improvement and growth.

Comprehensive Due Diligence Process:

The due diligence process in private equity is a multifaceted endeavor, encompassing a series of examinations and evaluations. Key components of the process include:

1. Financial Due Diligence:

◈ *Example*: In the case of Apex Capital's potential investment in XYZ Manufacturing, financial due diligence was extensive. Apex Capital's team, along with financial experts, scrutinized XYZ Manufacturing's financial statements, tax records, and forecasts. They conducted a deep analysis of revenue streams, cost structures, and cash flow. This process revealed opportunities for cost optimization and informed the negotiation of the purchase price.

2. Operational Due Diligence:

◈ *Example*: TerraNova Private Equity considered an investment in TerraTech, a manufacturing company. Operational due diligence involved an on-site visit to TerraTech's facilities. The team assessed production processes, supply chain efficiency, and quality control procedures. This evaluation highlighted areas for improvement and provided insights into operational strengths.

3. Legal and Regulatory Due Diligence:

◈ *Example*: In a potential investment in HealthCare Innovators, legal due diligence was critical. Legal experts reviewed contracts, intellectual property rights, and compliance with healthcare regulations. This process ensured that HealthCare Innovators had a solid legal foundation and minimized legal risks for the investment.

4. Market and Industry Analysis:

◈ *Example*: Nexus Equity Partners, specializing in healthcare investments, conducted market and industry analysis before investing in MediTech Solutions. This analysis included an assessment of market trends, competitive landscape, and growth potential. It confirmed that MediTech Solutions operated in a sector with robust growth prospects.

5. Technology and Intellectual Property Assessment:

◈ *Example*: TechVision Capital, focusing on technology investments, conducted a thorough assessment of the intellectual property portfolio of TechInnovate, a software development company. This assessment verified the strength of TechInnovate's intellectual property and its potential for competitive advantage.

6. Management Team Evaluation:

◈ *Example*: Vista Capital, considering an investment in InnovateTech, evaluated the management team. They assessed leadership qualities, industry expertise, and the team's ability to execute the company's growth strategy. This evaluation confirmed that InnovateTech had a capable and visionary leadership team.

Financial, Legal, and Operational Due Diligence

In the intricate world of private equity, the due diligence process is a pivotal stage in evaluating potential investments. It encompasses a thorough examination of financial, legal, and operational aspects, serving as the foundation upon which investment decisions are made. In this section, we delve into the critical components of financial, legal, and operational due diligence, emphasizing their significance and real-world examples.

Financial Due Diligence:

Financial due diligence is a comprehensive analysis of the target company's financial health, performance, and outlook. It involves meticulous examination of financial statements, historical financial data, and forecasts. Key aspects of financial due diligence include:

1. Financial Statement Analysis:

> ◈ *Example*: Apex Capital, considering an investment in XYZ Manufacturing, undertook financial due diligence. They rigorously analyzed XYZ Manufacturing's income statements, balance sheets, and cash flow statements over the past several years. This analysis revealed consistent revenue growth but also highlighted areas of cost inefficiency that could be optimized post-acquisition.

2. Cash Flow Assessment:

> ◈ *Example*: TerraNova Private Equity evaluated TerraTech's cash flow dynamics. They assessed the predictability of cash flows, working capital requirements, and capital expenditure needs. This assessment allowed TerraNova to understand the company's cash flow sustainability and opportunities for working capital improvements.

3. Revenue and Cost Analysis:

◈ *Example*: In the case of InnovateTech, Vista Capital conducted a detailed analysis of the company's revenue sources and cost structures. This examination revealed that while InnovateTech had diversified revenue streams, certain cost centers needed optimization, presenting opportunities for margin enhancement.

Legal Due Diligence:

Legal due diligence is a comprehensive review of the target company's legal affairs, contracts, intellectual property rights, and compliance with regulatory requirements. Key aspects of legal due diligence include:

1. Contract Review:

◈ *Example*: In their assessment of HealthCare Innovators, legal experts reviewed all contracts, including customer agreements, vendor contracts, and employment agreements. This process ensured that HealthCare Innovators had enforceable contracts in place, mitigating legal risks post-acquisition.

2. Intellectual Property Assessment:

◈ *Example*: TechVision Capital conducted a thorough assessment of TechInnovate's intellectual property portfolio. This assessment included patent and trademark reviews, ensuring that TechInnovate possessed valuable intellectual property assets that could provide a competitive advantage.

3. Regulatory Compliance:

◈ *Example*: In a potential investment in GreenEnergy Solutions, regulatory compliance was a key focus of legal due diligence. The review confirmed that GreenEnergy Solutions adhered to environmental regulations and obtained necessary permits, reducing the risk of regulatory issues.

Operational Due Diligence:

Operational due diligence evaluates the target company's operational efficiency, processes, and potential areas for improvement. Key aspects of operational due diligence include:

1. Facility Visits:

◈ *Example*: In the case of TerraTech, TerraNova Private Equity conducted on-site visits to assess manufacturing facilities. This firsthand evaluation allowed them to identify opportunities for production efficiency improvements and quality control enhancements.

2. Supply Chain Analysis:

◈ *Example*: Acme Private Equity, considering an investment in DistriTech, analyzed the company's supply chain. They identified opportunities to optimize procurement processes, reduce lead times, and enhance supplier relationships, ultimately improving operational efficiency.

3. Quality Control Evaluation:

◈ *Example*: In their due diligence for DistriTech, Acme Private Equity evaluated quality control procedures. They ensured that the company had robust quality assurance measures in place, reducing the risk of product defects and customer complaints.

dentifying and Mitigating Risks

In the realm of private equity, identifying and mitigating risks is paramount to safeguarding investments and ensuring favorable outcomes. Risk assessment is an integral part of the due diligence process, encompassing financial, legal, operational, and strategic aspects. In this section, we delve into the significance of risk identification and mitigation, emphasizing its practical application without the need for additional summaries or conclusions.

The Significance of Risk Identification:

Risk identification is a foundational step in the due diligence process. It entails a systematic examination of potential risks associated with the investment. Recognizing and understanding these risks is critical for several reasons:

1. **Informed Decision-Making**: Identifying risks enables private equity firms to make informed investment decisions. It ensures that potential pitfalls are acknowledged and considered when evaluating the investment's viability.

2. **Risk Mitigation**: Once identified, risks can be assessed and mitigated through proactive strategies and contingency plans. This reduces the likelihood of adverse outcomes.

3. **Alignment with Objectives**: Risk assessment helps ensure that the investment aligns with the private equity firm's objectives and risk tolerance. It ensures that the investment fits within the firm's portfolio and investment strategy.

4. Value Preservation: By addressing risks early in the due diligence process, private equity firms can protect the value they aim to create in the investment.

Practical Application: Identifying and Mitigating Risks:

Let's examine practical examples of risk identification and mitigation:

1. Market Risk:

◈ *Example*: Vista Capital considered an investment in TechInnovate, a software company. They identified market risk associated with the company's reliance on a single industry. To mitigate this risk, Vista Capital worked with TechInnovate's management to diversify the client base into multiple industries, reducing market concentration.

2. Legal Risk:

◈ *Example*: In their due diligence for HealthCare Innovators, legal experts identified potential legal risks related to compliance with healthcare regulations. To mitigate these risks, HealthCare Innovators implemented additional compliance measures and conducted regular internal audits.

3. Operational Risk:

◈ *Example*: TerraNova Private Equity recognized operational risks during their assessment of TerraTech's manufacturing facilities. To mitigate these risks, TerraNova Private Equity developed an operational improvement plan that included process optimization and quality control enhancements.

4. Financial Risk:

◈ *Example*: Apex Capital assessed financial risks in their potential investment in XYZ Manufacturing. They identified working capital challenges that could affect the company's liquidity. To mitigate this risk, Apex Capital provided a working capital injection as part of the acquisition, ensuring financial stability post-investment.

Chapter 6: Valuation and Pricing in Private Equity

Valuation Methods in Private Equity

In the intricate realm of private equity, valuation is a critical component that forms the foundation of investment decisions. Valuation methods are diverse and nuanced, each catering to the specific characteristics of the investment. In this section, we explore various valuation methods used in private equity, providing practical insights into their applications.

The Importance of Valuation:

Valuation in private equity is paramount for several reasons:

1. **Informed Decision-Making**: Valuation provides a basis for informed investment decisions, enabling private equity firms to gauge the potential return on investment.

2. **Negotiation and Deal Structuring**: Accurate valuation is vital during negotiations, allowing private equity firms to negotiate favorable terms and structure the deal to align with their objectives.

3. **Investor Confidence**: Transparent and accurate valuation builds investor confidence, ensuring that investors have a clear understanding of the value of their investments.

4. **Portfolio Performance Assessment**: Valuation allows private equity firms to track and assess the performance of their portfolio companies, facilitating strategic decisions regarding exits or further investment.

Common Valuation Methods in Private Equity:

Private equity firms employ various valuation methods, selecting the most appropriate based on the nature of the investment. Four common valuation methods include:

1. **Discounted Cash Flow (DCF) Analysis**:

◈ *Practical Insight*: Apex Capital utilized a DCF analysis to value a potential acquisition target, XYZ Manufacturing. By projecting the company's future cash flows and discounting them back to present value, they determined a fair valuation for the company. This method allowed them to negotiate a reasonable purchase price.

2. **Market Comparable Approach**:

◈ *Practical Insight*: Vista Capital utilized the market comparable approach when valuing TechInnovate, a software company. They compared TechInnovate's financial metrics, such as price-to-earnings ratios and enterprise values, with those of comparable publicly traded companies. This comparative analysis helped establish a reasonable valuation for TechInnovate.

3. **Transaction Comparable Approach**:

◈ *Practical Insight*: TerraNova Private Equity employed the transaction comparable approach when valuing TerraTech, a manufacturing company. They analyzed recent transactions in the manufacturing sector, considering the purchase price multiples and financial metrics. This approach provided valuable insights into the appropriate valuation for TerraTech.

4. **Asset-Based Valuation**:

◈ *Practical Insight*: Acme Private Equity considered an asset-based valuation for DistriTech, a distribution company. They assessed the company's assets, including tangible and intangible assets, and subtracted liabilities to determine the net asset value. This method aided in establishing a floor valuation for DistriTech.

Factors Influencing Valuation Method Selection:

The choice of valuation method depends on various factors, including:

◈ **Nature of the Business**: The industry and business model influence the choice of valuation method.

◈ **Stage of the Company**: Early-stage startups may require different valuation methods compared to mature companies.

◈ **Purpose of Valuation**: Whether it's for an acquisition, investment, or exit can influence the choice of the most appropriate valuation method.

◈ **Risk Profile**: The risk associated with the investment often guides the selection of a suitable valuation method.

Pricing Strategies in Deal Negotiations

In the intricate world of private equity, pricing strategies play a pivotal role during deal negotiations. These strategies are essential for arriving at a mutually acceptable purchase price, aligning the interests of both the buyer (private equity firm) and the seller (target company). In this section, we explore various pricing strategies employed in private equity deal negotiations, offering practical insights into their application.

The Importance of Pricing Strategies:

Pricing strategies are fundamental to deal negotiations in private equity for several reasons:

1. **Optimizing Returns**: Effective pricing strategies help private equity firms optimize returns on their investments. They ensure that the purchase price is aligned with the expected value creation potential.

2. **Negotiation Leverage**: The right pricing strategy can provide negotiation leverage, allowing private equity firms to secure favorable terms, including valuation multiples, earn-outs, and financing arrangements.

3. **Risk Mitigation**: Pricing strategies consider risk factors, ensuring that the purchase price reflects the level of risk associated with the investment.

4. **Investor Alignment**: Transparent and justifiable pricing strategies build investor confidence, aligning interests and expectations between private equity firms and their limited partners.

Common Pricing Strategies in Private Equity:

Private equity firms employ various pricing strategies, often tailored to the specific characteristics of the investment. Four common pricing strategies include:

1. **Earnings-Based Pricing:**

◈ *Practical Insight*: Apex Capital employed an earnings-based pricing strategy when negotiating the acquisition of XYZ Manufacturing. They used the company's historical and projected earnings to arrive at a purchase price that reflected the company's profitability. This strategy allowed Apex Capital to link the purchase price directly to the company's financial performance.

2. **Asset-Based Pricing**:

◈ *Practical Insight*: Acme Private Equity utilized an asset-based pricing strategy when negotiating the acquisition of DistriTech. They assessed the tangible and intangible assets of the company, including its brand and intellectual property. The purchase price was based on the net asset value, reflecting the underlying asset strength.

3. **Market Comparable Pricing**:

◈ *Practical Insight*: Vista Capital adopted a market comparable pricing strategy when negotiating the acquisition of TechInnovate. They compared the target company's valuation multiples, such as price-to-earnings ratios and price-to-sales ratios, to those of similar publicly traded companies. This strategy provided a market-driven benchmark for pricing.

4. **Strategic Value Pricing**:

◈ *Practical Insight*: TerraNova Private Equity applied a strategic value pricing strategy when negotiating the acquisition of TerraTech. They assessed the strategic value of the company within their portfolio, considering potential synergies and growth opportunities. This approach allowed TerraNova to justify a higher purchase price based on the strategic fit.

Factors Influencing Pricing Strategy:

The choice of pricing strategy is influenced by various factors, including:

◈ **Nature of the Investment**: The industry, growth potential, and risk profile of the target company influence the selection of a pricing strategy.

◈ **Market Conditions**: Market dynamics, including competition and supply-demand factors, play a role in determining the appropriate pricing strategy.

◈ **Seller Motivation**: Understanding the seller's motivation, such as a desire for a quick exit or a strategic partnership, can guide the choice of strategy.

◈ **Investment Thesis**: The alignment of the investment thesis with the pricing strategy ensures that the purchase price supports the intended value creation.

Determining Investment Entry Points

In the dynamic world of private equity, determining the right investment entry point is a pivotal aspect of the investment process. An entry point represents the timing and conditions under which a private equity firm initiates an investment. In this section, we explore the significance of identifying optimal entry points in private equity and provide practical insights into the factors and considerations involved.

The Significance of Entry Points:

Identifying the right entry point is crucial for several reasons:

1. **Risk Mitigation**: Optimal entry points consider market conditions, economic cycles, and risk factors, helping to mitigate potential downside risks.

2. **Return Optimization**: Entering an investment at an advantageous point can enhance potential returns, aligning with the private equity firm's value creation objectives.

3. **Portfolio Diversification**: Entry points play a role in diversifying a private equity firm's portfolio, balancing risk and return across various investments.

4. **Investor Expectations**: Private equity firms must align entry points with the expectations of their limited partners and investors, delivering on promised returns.

Factors Influencing Entry Point Determination:

Several factors influence the determination of investment entry points:

1. **Market Conditions**:

◈ *Practical Insight*: Apex Capital assessed market conditions when considering the entry point for an investment in XYZ Manufacturing. They monitored economic indicators, industry trends, and market sentiment to identify a favorable entry point during a market upswing, minimizing downside risk.

2. **Company Performance**:

◈ *Practical Insight*: TerraNova Private Equity considered TerraTech's performance when determining the entry point. They analyzed the company's historical financial performance and growth trajectory to identify a phase of consistent growth, signaling a suitable entry point.

3. **Valuation Multiples**:

◈ *Practical Insight*: Vista Capital evaluated TechInnovate's valuation multiples relative to the industry and market. By assessing whether the company was undervalued compared to peers, Vista Capital identified an attractive entry point.

4. **Strategic Fit**:

◈ *Practical Insight*: Acme Private Equity focused on the strategic fit of DistriTech when determining the entry point. They considered how the acquisition aligned with their overall portfolio strategy, identifying an entry point that enhanced their market presence.

Timing and Opportunity Assessment:

Determining the right entry point often involves assessing timing and opportunities. This assessment includes:

◈ **Macroeconomic Timing**: Evaluating economic cycles and market dynamics to identify favorable entry conditions.

◈ **Market Volatility**: Analyzing market volatility and fluctuations to pinpoint moments of reduced risk.

◈ **Industry Trends**: Monitoring industry-specific trends and disruptions that may create investment opportunities.

◈ **Competitive Landscape**: Assessing the competitive landscape to identify gaps or niches that align with the private equity firm's strategy.

Risk Management and Mitigation:

Private equity firms must also evaluate potential risks associated with their chosen entry point. This includes conducting due diligence to assess company-specific risks and macroeconomic risks that may impact the investment.

Case Studies in Valuation Challenges

Valuation challenges are inherent in the realm of private equity, where unique investment characteristics and dynamic market conditions often present complexities. In this section, we delve into real-world case studies that highlight the intricacies and challenges of valuing private equity investments, offering practical insights into how these challenges are navigated.

Case Study 1: The TechInnovate Conundrum:

TechInnovate, a technology startup, attracted the attention of Vista Capital, a private equity firm specializing in tech investments. The challenge lay in valuing a company with disruptive potential but limited historical financial data. Vista Capital faced the following hurdles:

◈ **Limited Financial History**: TechInnovate had limited revenue and profit history, making traditional valuation methods less applicable.

◈ **High Growth Expectations**: The tech sector was known for rapid growth, and TechInnovate was no exception.

Valuing a company with ambitious growth projections required careful consideration.

Solution: Vista Capital utilized a combination of methods, including discounted cash flow (DCF) analysis and market comps, but placed a strong emphasis on assessing the strategic value of TechInnovate. They factored in the potential for disruptive innovation and the scalability of the technology.

Case Study 2: The XYZ Manufacturing Turnaround:

Apex Capital considered an investment in *XYZ Manufacturing*, a company facing financial challenges. The valuation challenge was to determine a fair purchase price while accounting for turnaround efforts.

- **Operational Struggles**: XYZ Manufacturing was grappling with operational inefficiencies, leading to declining profitability.

- **Turnaround Efforts**: The management team at XYZ Manufacturing had outlined a comprehensive turnaround plan, with expectations of future profitability.

Solution: Apex Capital incorporated a risk-adjusted DCF analysis, factoring in the probability of the turnaround plan's success. They conducted thorough operational due diligence to identify areas for improvement and assess the feasibility of the turnaround strategy.

Case Study 3: DistriTech's Asset-Heavy Valuation:

Acme Private Equity evaluated *DistriTech*, a distribution company with a significant asset base. The challenge was to determine an accurate valuation considering the substantial tangible assets.

◈ **Asset Intensive**: DistriTech's valuation was complicated by its extensive tangible assets, including warehouses and inventory.

◈ **Asset Quality**: Assessing the quality and condition of assets was crucial for accurate valuation.

Solution: Acme Private Equity conducted an in-depth asset-based valuation, taking into account the condition, market value, and depreciation of assets. They also considered the company's growth potential beyond its assets, factoring in the strategic value.

Case Study 4: TerraTech's Industry Positioning:

TerraNova Private Equity assessed *TerraTech*, a manufacturing company operating in a niche market. The challenge was to value a company with limited comparable peers due to its specialized focus.

◈ **Niche Market**: TerraTech's niche market position made it challenging to find direct competitors for benchmarking.

◈ **Unique Products**: The company's unique products had limited comparables in the market.

Solution: TerraNova Private Equity relied on a combination of valuation methods, including the market comparable approach and strategic value assessment. They emphasized the company's market leadership in its niche and the potential for market expansion.

In conclusion, valuation challenges in private equity are diverse and require creative solutions. These case studies illustrate the importance of adaptability, a multi-faceted approach, and a keen understanding of the unique characteristics of each investment. Private equity firms must navigate these challenges effectively to make informed investment decisions and deliver value to their stakeholders.

Chapter 7: Financing Private Equity Deals

Leveraged Buyouts (LBOs) and Debt Financing

In the realm of private equity, financing is a critical aspect of executing deals. One of the most prevalent and distinctive forms of financing is the leveraged buyout (LBO). In this section, we explore LBOs and debt financing as essential tools for private equity firms, providing practical insights into their applications.

Leveraged Buyouts (LBOs) Defined:

A leveraged buyout (LBO) is a transaction in which a private equity firm acquires a company primarily using borrowed funds, often with a combination of equity capital from the private equity fund and debt financing. LBOs are a common strategy in the private equity industry for several reasons:

1. **Enhanced Return Potential**: By using leverage (borrowed funds), private equity firms can amplify their returns on investment. This can lead to significant wealth creation if the acquired company's value increases over time.

2. **Capital Efficiency**: LBOs allow private equity firms to maximize the use of their capital by using debt to fund a substantial portion of the purchase price. This frees up capital for additional investments.

3. **Alignment of Interests**: LBOs align the interests of the private equity firm and the company's management, as both parties often have an equity stake in the business.

4. **Operational Improvements**: Private equity firms typically implement operational improvements in the acquired company to enhance its value and generate returns for investors.

Debt Financing in LBOs:

Debt financing is a cornerstone of LBOs. Private equity firms utilize various forms of debt, such as bank loans, bonds, and mezzanine financing, to fund the acquisition. Here's how it works:

- **Senior Debt**: This is typically the primary form of debt in an LBO. It's secured by the assets of the acquired company and has a higher priority in repayment.

- **Mezzanine Financing**: Mezzanine debt is subordinated to senior debt but ranks higher than equity. It often carries higher interest rates to compensate for the added risk.

- **High-Yield Bonds**: Private equity firms may issue high-yield bonds to raise capital for the LBO. These bonds have higher interest rates but offer more flexibility than bank loans.

Practical Insight:

Let's consider a practical example of an LBO and debt financing:

- *Scenario*: TerraNova Private Equity is interested in acquiring GreenTech Solutions, a renewable energy company. The purchase price is $100 million. TerraNova plans to fund the acquisition using a combination of equity capital from their fund and debt financing.

- *Financing Structure*: TerraNova decides to use an LBO structure. They contribute $30 million in equity capital from their fund and secure $70 million in senior debt from a bank. This debt will be backed by the assets and cash flows of GreenTech Solutions.

◈ *Debt Terms*: The senior debt has a term of seven years with an interest rate of 5%. TerraNova anticipates that they can improve GreenTech Solutions' operations and generate enough cash flow to service the debt.

◈ *Potential Returns*: If TerraNova successfully enhances the value of GreenTech Solutions, the returns on their $30 million equity investment can be substantial, as they only put up a fraction of the purchase price.

Equity Financing and Co-Investment Structures

In the world of private equity, financing deals isn't solely reliant on debt. Equity financing, often in conjunction with co-investment structures, plays a vital role in structuring transactions. In this section, we explore equity financing and co-investment structures, shedding light on their significance and practical applications.

Equity Financing Defined:

Equity financing in private equity refers to the provision of capital by investors, typically private equity funds and their limited partners, to acquire ownership stakes in companies. Unlike debt financing, equity financing does not involve borrowing funds that need to be repaid with interest. Instead, equity investors become shareholders in the acquired company.

Co-Investment Structures:

Co-investment structures are arrangements in which external investors, often the limited partners of a private equity fund, have the opportunity to directly invest alongside the fund in specific transactions. Co-investors share the risk and potential returns with the private equity fund.

Significance of Equity Financing and Co-Investment:

1. **Capital Injection:** Equity financing provides the necessary capital to fund acquisitions, growth initiatives, and operational improvements within portfolio companies.

2. **Alignment of Interests:** Co-investment structures align the interests of the fund manager and limited partners, ensuring that both parties share in the success of individual transactions.

3. **Risk Sharing:** Co-investors share the financial risk associated with specific investments, which can be reassuring for the fund manager and offer diversification to limited partners.

4. **Enhanced Returns:** Successful transactions generate returns for both the private equity fund and co-investors, potentially amplifying overall fund performance.

Practical Insight:

Consider a practical example of equity financing and co-investment:

◈ *Scenario:* Apex Capital is a private equity firm seeking to acquire GreenEco, a company specializing in environmentally friendly consumer products. The purchase price is $80 million, and Apex Capital intends to use both equity financing and co-investment.

◈ *Financing Structure*: Apex Capital contributes $40 million from its private equity fund as equity financing. Simultaneously, the firm offers its limited partners the opportunity to co-invest an additional $20 million directly in the GreenEco acquisition, sharing in the ownership and returns.

◈ *Alignment of Interests*: The co-investment structure aligns the interests of Apex Capital and its limited partners. Both parties aim to maximize the success of the GreenEco acquisition, as they will share in the financial rewards.

◈ *Risk Mitigation*: By allowing limited partners to co-invest, Apex Capital spreads the financial risk associated with the transaction. This reduces the fund's exposure and provides diversification for investors.

◈ *Returns*: If the GreenEco acquisition proves successful and the company's value increases, both Apex Capital and the co-investors benefit from enhanced returns on their investments.

Structuring Capital Stacks in Private Equity

In the intricate landscape of private equity, structuring capital stacks is a fundamental aspect of deal execution. A capital stack refers to the composition of capital, both equity and debt, used to finance an acquisition or investment. In this section, we delve into the art of structuring capital stacks in private equity, offering practical insights into its significance and methods.

The Significance of Capital Stacks:

Structuring capital stacks is essential for several reasons:

1. **Risk Management**: The composition of the capital stack determines the risk profile of the investment. Balancing equity and debt can help mitigate financial risk.

2. **Return Optimization**: A well-structured capital stack can optimize returns. Using leverage through debt financing can amplify potential returns if the investment performs well.

3. **Flexibility**: Different investments may require varying capital structures. Structuring the capital stack allows private equity firms to tailor financing to the unique characteristics of each deal.

Components of a Capital Stack:

A typical capital stack in private equity comprises multiple layers, including:

1. **Senior Debt**: This is often the primary layer and consists of secured loans provided by banks or financial institutions. Senior debt has a priority claim on the company's assets and cash flows.

2. **Mezzanine Debt**: Mezzanine debt is subordinate to senior debt but ranks higher than equity. It typically carries higher interest rates and may include features such as warrants or equity kickers.

3. **Equity**: Equity capital comes from the private equity fund, limited partners, and potentially co-investors. Equity investors become shareholders in the acquired company.

Practical Insight:

Let's consider a practical example of structuring a capital stack:

- *Scenario*: TerraNova Private Equity is pursuing the acquisition of TerraSolutions, a technology services company, with a purchase price of $120 million.

- *Capital Stack Structure*:

- TerraNova commits $40 million in equity capital from its private equity fund, representing one-third of the purchase price.

- To finance the remaining $80 million, TerraNova secures senior debt of $60 million from a bank. The senior debt is secured by TerraSolutions' assets and cash flows.

- TerraNova also utilizes mezzanine financing to cover the remaining $20 million. This mezzanine debt carries a higher interest rate than the senior debt but provides flexibility in the capital structure.

- *Risk and Return*: The capital stack balances risk and return. By using debt financing, TerraNova can potentially amplify returns on its $40 million equity investment if TerraSolutions performs well.

Financing Alternatives in Private Equity

In the realm of private equity, financing is not a one-size-fits-all endeavor. Beyond traditional capital stacks, private equity firms have a range of financing alternatives at their disposal to structure deals creatively and effectively. In this section, we explore these financing alternatives and their practical applications.

Exploring Financing Alternatives:

1. **Preferred Equity**: Preferred equity represents a hybrid form of financing that combines elements of both equity and debt. Investors in preferred equity have a senior claim over common equity but do not typically hold the same voting rights. Private equity firms can utilize preferred equity to infuse capital into an investment while offering investors a degree of protection and income in the form of dividends.

   Practical Insight: Apex Capital structures a deal for an emerging tech startup by offering preferred equity to outside investors. This allows the startup to access necessary capital while giving investors a preference in the event of liquidation or dividend distribution.

2. **Convertible Debt**: Convertible debt is a form of financing that starts as debt but can be converted into equity at a predetermined conversion ratio. It provides companies with immediate debt capital while offering the potential for investors to convert to equity when the company's valuation increases.

   Practical Insight: TerraNova Private Equity invests in a promising biotech company using convertible debt. If the company's drug development leads to significant value appreciation, the debt can convert into equity, allowing TerraNova to participate in the upside.

3. **Royalty Financing**: In certain industries like healthcare and technology, royalty financing allows private equity firms to provide capital in exchange for a share of future revenues.

This innovative approach aligns the interests of the investor and the company in achieving revenue growth.

Practical Insight: Acme Private Equity employs royalty financing when investing in a pharmaceutical firm. In return for their capital, Acme receives a percentage of the company's future drug sales, offering potential long-term revenue.

4. **Unitranche Financing**: Unitranche financing combines senior and mezzanine debt into a single loan facility. It simplifies the debt structure, streamlines negotiations, and offers flexibility in terms of repayment. Private equity firms can leverage unitranche financing for acquisitions that require a straightforward debt arrangement.

Practical Insight: Vista Capital secures unitranche financing when acquiring a mid-sized manufacturing company. This approach simplifies the financing process and provides efficient access to the required capital.

5. **Revenue-Based Financing**: Revenue-based financing involves investors providing capital in exchange for a percentage of a company's future revenue. This financing method is often used by startups and growth-stage companies.

Practical Insight: Apex Capital supports a technology startup with revenue-based financing. In this arrangement, the startup repays the investment based on its future revenue, which aligns the investor's returns with the company's success.

Customized Financing for Optimal Results:

The choice of financing alternative in private equity depends on the unique characteristics of each investment and the preferences of investors. Customized financing structures can optimize capital efficiency, align interests, and enhance the overall success of private equity deals. As the private equity landscape evolves, innovative financing approaches continue to offer new avenues for value creation.

Chapter 8: Private Equity Legal and Regulatory Framework

Legal Structures for Private Equity Funds

Within the world of private equity, the legal and regulatory framework is a critical foundation that shapes how funds operate and the relationships they maintain with investors. In this section, we explore the various legal structures employed by private equity funds, shedding light on their significance and practical applications.

Fund Structures in Private Equity:

Private equity funds are typically organized as limited partnerships or limited liability companies (LLCs). These structures serve distinct purposes and offer specific benefits:

1. **Limited Partnership (LP):**

   ◈ *Practical Insight*: Apex Capital establishes its latest private equity fund, Apex Equity Partners Fund III, as a limited partnership. This structure allows them to have general partners (the fund managers) who manage the operations and limited partners (the investors) who provide the capital but have limited liability.

2. **Limited Liability Company (LLC):**

   ◈ *Practical Insight*: TerraNova Private Equity opts for an LLC structure when launching TerraNova Growth Fund. The LLC structure provides operational flexibility and a simplified management structure, allowing the fund managers to tailor governance to suit the fund's objectives.

Master-Feeder Structures:

In some cases, private equity funds utilize master-feeder structures to attract different classes of investors. In this setup, multiple feeder funds pool capital into a master fund, which then makes investments on behalf of all the feeder funds. This structure can accommodate different types of investors, such as taxable and tax-exempt entities.

> ◈ *Practical Insight*: Acme Private Equity employs a master-feeder structure for its fund family. The Acme Growth Fund, Acme Opportunity Fund, and Acme Income Fund are feeder funds that channel their investments into the Acme Master Fund. This approach caters to the diverse investor preferences within their investor base.

Fund Domicile:

Private equity funds can be domiciled in various jurisdictions, depending on legal and tax considerations. Common domiciles include the United States, the Cayman Islands, Luxembourg, and the British Virgin Islands. The choice of domicile impacts regulatory oversight, taxation, and investor reporting requirements.

> ◈ *Practical Insight*: Vista Capital opts to domicile its Vista Technology Fund in the Cayman Islands. This jurisdiction offers tax efficiency and a streamlined regulatory framework for international investors.

Regulatory Compliance:

Private equity funds must adhere to regulatory requirements imposed by relevant authorities. Compliance includes adhering to securities laws, anti-money laundering (AML) regulations, and know-your-customer (KYC) procedures. Additionally, funds often engage compliance officers and legal counsel to navigate complex regulatory landscapes.

- *Practical Insight*: TerraNova Private Equity maintains a robust compliance team to ensure adherence to regulatory requirements across different jurisdictions where they operate. This team oversees AML checks, KYC procedures, and reporting obligations to relevant authorities.

Regulatory Compliance and Reporting

In the dynamic landscape of private equity, adherence to regulatory compliance and robust reporting practices are paramount. In this section, we delve into the critical aspects of regulatory compliance and reporting that private equity firms must navigate to ensure transparency, trust, and adherence to legal requirements.

Compliance with Securities Laws:

Private equity funds operate within a framework of securities laws and regulations that vary by jurisdiction. Compliance with these laws is essential to maintain the integrity of the investment process and protect investors' interests. Key considerations include:

- **Accurate Disclosure**: Private equity firms must provide accurate and complete disclosures to investors, detailing fund terms, risks, and potential conflicts of interest.

- **Fundraising Compliance**: Adherence to regulations regarding the solicitation and acceptance of capital from investors is crucial. Private equity firms must ensure that fundraising activities comply with securities laws.

◈ **Investor Suitability**: Firms need to assess the suitability of investors to participate in private equity funds, ensuring that they meet specific criteria, such as accredited investor status.

Anti-Money Laundering (AML) and Know Your Customer (KYC) Practices:

AML and KYC procedures are integral to maintaining the integrity of private equity investments. Firms must implement robust AML policies and conduct due diligence on investors to prevent money laundering and illicit activities. This includes:

◈ **Client Identification**: Verification of the identity of investors and beneficial owners to prevent unauthorized access to funds.

◈ **Source of Funds**: Thorough investigation of the source of funds to detect and prevent illegal or fraudulent activities.

◈ **Suspicious Activity Reporting**: Establishing procedures to identify and report suspicious transactions to the relevant authorities.

Regulatory Reporting:

Private equity firms are often required to submit periodic reports to regulatory bodies, investors, and other stakeholders. These reports include:

◈ **Financial Statements**: Detailed financial statements that provide a comprehensive view of the fund's financial performance, including income, expenses, and net asset value.

◈ **Operational Reports**: Reports on the fund's operations, such as investment activity, portfolio performance, and compliance with fund documents.

◈ **Tax Reporting**: Compliance with tax regulations and reporting obligations, both at the fund and investor levels.

Transparency and Investor Communications:

Maintaining transparency with investors is essential in private equity. This includes:

◈ **Quarterly Reports**: Regularly providing investors with quarterly reports that detail fund performance, investment activity, and financial metrics.

◈ **Fund Updates**: Keeping investors informed about significant developments, such as changes in fund strategy, key personnel, or fund terms.

◈ **Conflicts of Interest**: Disclosing any conflicts of interest that may arise during the course of fund management.

Global Regulatory Considerations:

Private equity firms operating across borders must navigate a complex web of global regulations. Each jurisdiction may have unique requirements related to investor relations, reporting, and tax compliance. Staying informed and ensuring adherence to these regulations is crucial.

Practical Insight:

Vista Capital, a global private equity firm, exemplifies best practices in regulatory compliance and reporting. They maintain a dedicated compliance team that monitors regulatory changes across multiple jurisdictions where they operate. This team ensures that Vista Capital's funds adhere to securities laws, implement robust AML and KYC procedures, and deliver comprehensive and transparent reporting to investors.

Key Legal Documents in Private Equity Transactions

In the intricate world of private equity, transactions are governed by a multitude of legal documents that establish the rights, obligations, and expectations of all parties involved. In this section, we explore some of the key legal documents that play a pivotal role in structuring and executing private equity transactions.

1. Limited Partnership Agreement (LPA):

The Limited Partnership Agreement (LPA) is a foundational document that governs the relationship between the general partner (private equity firm) and limited partners (investors) in a private equity fund. The LPA outlines the fund's structure, investment strategy, terms, and the rights and responsibilities of each party. It covers critical aspects such as capital contributions, profit sharing, management fees, and carried interest.

2. Subscription Agreement:

The Subscription Agreement is a contract between the investor and the private equity fund. It outlines the terms and conditions of the investor's commitment to provide capital to the fund. This document includes details about the amount of capital to be contributed, payment schedule, representations and warranties, and compliance with regulatory requirements.

3. Private Placement Memorandum (PPM):

The Private Placement Memorandum is a comprehensive disclosure document provided to potential investors. It offers a detailed overview of the fund's investment strategy, risks, fees, and terms. The PPM plays a crucial role in ensuring that investors have access to all necessary information to make informed investment decisions.

4. Side Letters:

Side letters are agreements between the private equity fund and specific investors that modify or augment the terms outlined in the LPA or PPM. These letters may grant certain investors preferential rights, fee structures, or reporting requirements based on their individual circumstances or requests.

5. Co-Investment Agreements:

Co-Investment Agreements are contracts between the private equity fund and investors who opt to directly participate in specific transactions alongside the fund. These agreements define the terms and conditions of co-investment, including the allocation of profits and sharing of expenses.

6. Management Services Agreement:

In cases where the private equity firm provides management services to portfolio companies, a Management Services Agreement is executed. This document outlines the scope of services, fees, and the duration of the management arrangement.

7. Acquisition Documents:

When a private equity firm acquires a portfolio company, a range of transaction-specific agreements come into play. These include Purchase Agreements, Stock or Asset Purchase Agreements, and Escrow

Agreements. These documents detail the terms of the acquisition, representations, warranties, and the conditions of closing.

8. Exit Documents:

When it's time to exit an investment, documents such as Sale Agreements, Stock Purchase Agreements, or Merger Agreements are used to formalize the sale of the portfolio company. These agreements outline the terms of the sale, purchase price, and conditions for closing.

Practical Insight:

TerraNova Private Equity exemplifies the meticulous use of legal documents in private equity transactions. When launching TerraNova Growth Fund II, they diligently drafted LPAs, Subscription Agreements, and a comprehensive PPM. Throughout the fund's life cycle, they utilize side letters to accommodate specific investor requests while ensuring compliance with the core fund documents.

Tax Implications in Private Equity

Navigating the tax landscape is a pivotal aspect of private equity transactions. Tax considerations can significantly impact the structure, profitability, and compliance of these investments. In this section, we delve into the key tax implications that private equity firms must address in their operations.

1. Structuring Tax-Efficient Vehicles:

Private equity funds often choose specific legal structures and domiciles to optimize tax efficiency. Common structures include limited partnerships (LPs), limited liability companies (LLCs), and master-feeder structures. Domicile selection can also impact tax liability. For example, funds domiciled in the Cayman Islands may benefit from tax neutrality.

2. Taxation of Carried Interest:

Carried interest, or "carry," represents the share of profits that private equity fund managers receive as compensation. The tax treatment of carried interest varies by jurisdiction and can have a significant impact on fund managers' tax liability. It's often subject to capital gains tax rates, which are generally lower than ordinary income tax rates.

3. Flow-Through Taxation:

Many private equity vehicles, such as LPs and LLCs, are structured as pass-through entities for tax purposes. This means that income and gains flow through to investors, who report them on their individual tax returns. This flow-through structure can provide tax advantages, such as avoiding double taxation at the fund and investor levels.

4. Tax Reporting and Compliance:

Private equity firms must adhere to strict tax reporting and compliance requirements. This includes preparing and filing tax returns, providing tax documents to investors, and ensuring compliance with tax regulations in multiple jurisdictions. Compliance is particularly complex for international funds with investors and investments in various countries.

5. Tax Due Diligence:

Before acquiring a portfolio company, private equity firms conduct tax due diligence to assess potential tax liabilities and identify opportunities for tax optimization. This process involves examining the company's historical tax returns, positions, and potential exposure to tax risks.

6. Structuring Acquisitions and Exits for Tax Efficiency:

The structure of acquisitions and exits can impact the tax implications of private equity investments. Private equity firms may use strategies such as leveraged buyouts (LBOs) or mergers and acquisitions (M&A) to optimize tax efficiency, such as capital gains treatment upon exit.

7. Value-Added Tax (VAT) and Sales Tax:

In some jurisdictions, VAT or sales tax may apply to certain transactions, including the sale of goods or services by portfolio companies. Private equity firms must consider and comply with these indirect tax regulations.

Practical Insight:

Apex Capital, a global private equity firm, demonstrates meticulous attention to tax implications. When structuring Apex Global Fund, they opted for a limited partnership structure with flow-through taxation to provide tax advantages to their international investor base. The firm also engages tax experts to conduct thorough due diligence on portfolio companies, ensuring they maximize tax efficiency during acquisitions and exits.

Chapter 9: Private Equity Performance and Measurement

Performance Metrics in Private Equity

Assessing the performance of private equity investments requires a distinct set of metrics and methodologies. In this section, we explore the key performance metrics used to evaluate the success and profitability of private equity investments.

1. Internal Rate of Return (IRR):

The Internal Rate of Return (IRR) is a fundamental metric in private equity. It measures the annualized rate of return that an investor can expect to earn from their investment. The IRR accounts for the time value of money and considers both cash inflows (distributions) and outflows (contributions) over the life of the investment.

2. Multiple of Invested Capital (MOIC):

The Multiple of Invested Capital (MOIC) compares the total distributions received from an investment to the total capital contributed. It represents how many times the original investment has been returned. For example, an MOIC of 2.0 means the investment has doubled in value.

3. Public Market Equivalent (PME):

The Public Market Equivalent (PME) measures the relative performance of a private equity investment compared to investing in a public market index, such as the S&P 500. PME accounts for the illiquidity and longer holding periods of private equity investments.

4. Time-Weighted Return:

Time-Weighted Return calculates the average rate of return for each investment period within the private equity fund, considering the size and duration of each investment. It provides a more accurate reflection of investment performance when funds have multiple investments with varying lifecycles.

5. Cash Flow Metrics:

Cash flow metrics assess the timing and magnitude of cash inflows and outflows. They include metrics such as:

- **Distributions to Paid-in Capital (DPI):** Measures the ratio of distributions to the total capital contributed.

- **Residual Value to Paid-in Capital (RVPI):** Measures the ratio of the remaining value of the investment to the total capital contributed.

- **Total Value to Paid-in Capital (TVPI):** Combines DPI and RVPI to assess the total value created relative to the capital invested.

6. Net Asset Value (NAV):

Net Asset Value represents the total value of the fund's assets minus its liabilities. It provides a snapshot of the fund's value at a specific point in time and is commonly used for reporting purposes.

7. Benchmarking:

Benchmarking involves comparing the performance of a private equity fund to relevant benchmarks, such as industry peers or market indices. Benchmarking helps investors assess how a fund's returns compare to similar investments.

Practical Insight:

TerraNova Private Equity employs a comprehensive approach to performance measurement. When evaluating the performance of TerraNova Growth Fund II, they calculate key metrics like IRR, MOIC, and TVPI to provide investors with a holistic view of the fund's success. Benchmarking against industry peers and public market indices further aids in assessing the fund's relative performance.

Measuring Portfolio Company Success

In the realm of private equity, success is not solely determined by the performance of the entire fund; it also hinges on the success of individual portfolio companies. In this section, we explore the methodologies and key performance indicators used to measure the success and value creation of portfolio companies within a private equity fund.

1. Earnings Before Interest, Taxes, Depreciation, and Amortization (EBITDA):

EBITDA is a fundamental financial metric used to assess the operating performance and profitability of a portfolio company. Private equity firms often aim to enhance a company's EBITDA during their ownership, as it can contribute to increased valuation and returns upon exit.

2. Revenue Growth:

Revenue growth is a critical indicator of a portfolio company's success. Private equity investors seek to accelerate revenue growth through various strategies, such as expanding market share, entering new markets, or launching new products or services.

3. Operating Margin Improvement:

Operating margin, which measures a company's profitability relative to its revenue, is closely monitored. Private equity firms often work to improve operating margins by optimizing costs, streamlining operations, and implementing efficiency measures.

4. Cash Flow Generation:

Positive cash flow is essential for the sustainability and growth of portfolio companies. Private equity investors focus on generating strong cash flows to support ongoing operations, investments in growth initiatives, and debt servicing.

5. Return on Investment (ROI):

ROI measures the profitability of an investment relative to its cost. Private equity firms assess the ROI of portfolio companies to evaluate the efficiency of capital allocation and the success of their value-creation strategies.

6. Customer Retention and Acquisition:

The ability to retain existing customers and acquire new ones is indicative of a portfolio company's market position and growth potential. Private equity investors often work with management teams to develop customer-centric strategies.

7. Debt Reduction:

Reducing excessive debt and optimizing the capital structure of portfolio companies is a common goal for private equity investors. Lower debt levels can enhance financial stability and flexibility.

8. Strategic Initiatives:

Private equity firms often collaborate with portfolio company management to execute strategic initiatives. These initiatives can include mergers and acquisitions, geographic expansion, diversification, and technology adoption.

9. Key Performance Indicators (KPIs):

Private equity investors establish KPIs tailored to each portfolio company's industry and objectives. These KPIs can cover areas such as customer satisfaction, market share, inventory turnover, and employee productivity.

Practical Insight:

Apex Capital, a private equity firm specializing in technology investments, measures the success of its portfolio companies through a combination of financial metrics and strategic initiatives. For example, when evaluating the success of a software company in its portfolio, Apex considers factors such as EBITDA growth, customer acquisition rates, and the successful rollout of new product features.

Benchmarking Private Equity Returns

Benchmarking is a crucial practice in private equity that enables investors and fund managers to assess the performance of their investments against relevant industry standards and peers. In this section, we explore the significance of benchmarking private equity returns and the methodologies involved.

1. Comparing to Public Market Indices:

One common approach to benchmarking private equity returns is to compare them to public market indices. Private equity investments are typically illiquid and have longer holding periods than publicly traded securities. Thus, benchmarking against relevant indices, such as the S&P 500 or Russell 2000, helps investors assess how private equity returns compare to the broader market.

2. Using Private Equity-Specific Indices:

To provide a more accurate benchmark for private equity, investors and fund managers can turn to specialized private equity indices. These indices track the performance of private equity investments and are tailored to the asset class's characteristics, such as illiquidity and longer investment horizons. Examples include the Cambridge Associates Private Equity Index and the Burgiss Private Equity Indices.

3. Peer Group Comparison:

Benchmarking against a peer group of private equity firms with similar strategies and focuses can offer valuable insights. Private equity firms often assess their returns in comparison to peers that operate in the same sectors or geographic regions.

4. Vintage Year Analysis:

Private equity returns can vary significantly based on the vintage year of the fund. Vintage year analysis involves comparing the performance of a specific fund to the performance of other funds raised in the same year. This approach considers the economic and market conditions prevailing during that time.

5. Quartile Rankings:

Quartile rankings categorize private equity funds into four quartiles based on their performance relative to peers. This ranking system allows investors to see whether a fund falls into the top quartile, indicating superior performance, or lower quartiles, indicating underperformance.

6. Risk-Adjusted Metrics:

To account for risk, investors often use risk-adjusted metrics such as the Sharpe ratio or the Jensen's alpha. These metrics assess whether the returns generated by a private equity fund are commensurate with the level of risk undertaken.

7. Time-Weighted Return Analysis:

Time-weighted return analysis evaluates a fund's performance over different time periods, taking into account the impact of investment inflows and outflows. This approach provides a more accurate representation of performance over time.

Practical Insight:

Vista Capital, a private equity firm specializing in technology investments, regularly benchmarks its funds against relevant public market indices, such as the NASDAQ Composite Index. Additionally, they use vintage year analysis to assess the performance of their funds in the context of the economic conditions during the fund's inception.

Investor Reporting and Transparency

In the world of private equity, investor reporting and transparency play a pivotal role in maintaining trust, fostering long-term relationships, and ensuring that investors are well-informed about the performance of their investments. In this section, we explore the significance of investor reporting and transparency practices within private equity.

1. Timely and Comprehensive Reporting:

Private equity firms are responsible for providing investors with regular, clear, and comprehensive reports on the performance of their investments. These reports typically include financial statements, updates on portfolio companies, and information on fund activities.

2. Customized Reporting:

Investor reporting is often tailored to meet the specific needs and preferences of different investors. Some investors may require more detailed information, while others may prefer summarized reports. Private equity firms strive to accommodate these preferences.

3. Frequency of Reporting:

Reporting frequencies can vary but often include quarterly or semi-annual updates. These reports help investors track the progress of their investments over time and make informed decisions.

4. Performance Metrics:

Investor reports typically include key performance metrics, such as Internal Rate of Return (IRR), Multiple of Invested Capital (MOIC), and cash flow information. These metrics provide insights into the financial performance and value creation of the fund.

5. Portfolio Company Updates:

Investors expect updates on individual portfolio companies, including financial performance, strategic initiatives, and any significant developments. Transparent communication regarding portfolio companies' successes and challenges fosters trust and accountability.

6. Fund Expenses and Fees:

Transparency regarding fund expenses and fees is essential. Private equity firms provide detailed breakdowns of management fees, carried interest, and any other fees charged to the fund. Investors appreciate clarity on how fees impact their returns.

7. Performance Attribution:

Investor reporting often includes performance attribution analysis, which breaks down the sources of fund returns. This analysis helps investors understand which investments and strategies contributed most to fund performance.

8. Risk and Mitigation:

Reports should also include discussions on risk factors and the strategies employed to mitigate these risks. Transparency about potential challenges and how they are managed enhances investor confidence.

9. Disclosure of Conflicts of Interest:

Private equity firms disclose any conflicts of interest that may arise in the course of managing the fund. This transparency allows investors to assess the impact of potential conflicts on their investments.

Practical Insight:

TerraNova Private Equity is renowned for its commitment to investor reporting and transparency. When communicating with investors in TerraNova Growth Fund II, they provide comprehensive reports that include financial performance, portfolio company updates, and discussions on risk and mitigation strategies. This approach fosters a strong sense of trust and partnership between the firm and its investors.

Chapter 10: Emerging Trends in Private Equity

ESG Considerations in Private Equity

In recent years, Environmental, Social, and Governance (ESG) considerations have gained significant prominence in the private equity industry. ESG factors encompass a broad range of criteria that assess a company's impact on the environment, society, and corporate governance. Private equity firms are increasingly recognizing the importance of integrating ESG principles into their investment strategies. In this section, we explore the growing significance of ESG considerations in private equity.

1. Environmental Sustainability:

Private equity firms are placing greater emphasis on investing in companies that prioritize environmental sustainability. This includes evaluating a portfolio company's carbon footprint, energy efficiency, and environmental impact. Firms may seek opportunities in industries focused on renewable energy, clean technology, and resource conservation.

2. Social Responsibility:

ESG considerations extend to a portfolio company's social impact. Private equity investors assess factors such as labor practices, workplace diversity, and community engagement. Companies that promote fair labor conditions, diversity and inclusion, and community development are increasingly attractive to investors.

3. Governance Practices:

Corporate governance is a critical ESG component. Private equity firms look for companies with strong governance practices, transparent financial reporting, and ethical leadership. They may encourage portfolio companies to enhance board diversity, adopt robust corporate governance structures, and establish effective risk management processes.

4. Impact Investing:

Impact investing focuses on generating positive social and environmental outcomes alongside financial returns. Private equity firms are launching impact-focused funds that target companies aligned with specific ESG goals, such as improving healthcare access, reducing carbon emissions, or addressing social inequalities.

5. ESG Due Diligence:

ESG due diligence is becoming a standard practice during the investment process. Private equity firms assess potential investments for ESG risks and opportunities. This diligence includes evaluating a company's adherence to ESG regulations, potential reputational risks, and alignment with the United Nations Sustainable Development Goals (SDGs).

6. Reporting and Disclosure:

Private equity firms are improving their ESG reporting and disclosure practices. They provide investors with ESG-related performance metrics, such as carbon emissions reductions, diversity metrics, and community impact assessments. Enhanced reporting enables investors to assess the tangible impact of ESG initiatives.

7. Regulatory Compliance:

As governments and regulatory bodies introduce ESG-related regulations, private equity firms are adapting to ensure compliance. They stay informed about evolving ESG reporting requirements and integrate them into their investment strategies.

8. Long-Term Value Creation:

Private equity investors recognize that ESG considerations are not just about ethical investing but also contribute to long-term value creation. Companies that effectively manage ESG risks and opportunities are more likely to achieve sustainable growth and resilience in an evolving business landscape.

Practical Insight:

Vista Capital, a private equity firm specializing in technology investments, has incorporated ESG considerations into its investment thesis. They actively seek technology companies that address environmental challenges, promote diversity in the tech industry, and contribute to social causes. By aligning their investments with ESG principles, Vista Capital aims to drive positive change while generating financial returns.

The Role of Technology in Private Equity

Technology is transforming the landscape of private equity, revolutionizing the way firms operate, make investment decisions, and add value to portfolio companies. In this section, we delve into the profound impact of technology on the private equity industry.

1. Data Analytics and Due Diligence:

Data analytics is at the forefront of private equity decision-making. Advanced data analytics tools enable firms to conduct comprehensive due diligence on potential investments. They analyze vast datasets to assess market trends, competitive landscapes, and the financial health of target companies. This data-driven approach enhances investment selection and risk assessment.

2. Artificial Intelligence (AI) and Machine Learning:

AI and machine learning algorithms are being applied to identify investment opportunities and optimize portfolio company performance. Predictive analytics models can evaluate the potential success of specific investments and suggest strategies for enhancing operational efficiency within portfolio companies.

3. Deal Sourcing and Screening:

Technology platforms and data aggregators streamline deal sourcing by providing access to a vast network of potential investment opportunities. Private equity firms use these platforms to identify companies that align with their investment criteria, significantly expanding their deal flow.

4. Portfolio Management:

Technology tools and platforms assist private equity firms in actively managing their portfolio companies. They offer real-time performance tracking, financial modeling, and strategic planning capabilities. This technology-driven approach allows for quicker decision-making and better portfolio optimization.

5. Cybersecurity and Data Protection:

Given the sensitive nature of financial data, private equity firms invest heavily in cybersecurity measures. They employ advanced encryption, intrusion detection systems, and employee training to safeguard data against cyber threats and breaches.

6. Virtual Data Rooms (VDRs):

Virtual data rooms have become a staple in due diligence and deal execution. These secure online platforms enable the efficient exchange of confidential documents and data between buyers, sellers, and advisors, streamlining the deal-making process.

7. Blockchain Technology:

Blockchain technology is gaining traction in private equity for improving transparency, reducing fraud, and streamlining administrative processes such as fund administration and compliance tracking.

8. Portfolio Company Growth:

Private equity firms leverage technology to drive growth within portfolio companies. This includes implementing digital marketing strategies, optimizing supply chain management, and adopting data-driven decision-making processes.

9. Reporting and Communication:

Investor reporting has also benefited from technology. Online portals and secure communication platforms facilitate seamless reporting and communication between private equity firms and their investors.

10. Regulatory Compliance:

Technology tools aid in ensuring regulatory compliance by automating compliance checks and reporting requirements. They help private equity firms navigate complex regulatory landscapes efficiently.

Practical Insight:

TerraNova Private Equity exemplifies the integration of technology into private equity operations. They employ AI-driven data analytics to identify investment opportunities with growth potential. Additionally, they utilize technology platforms for portfolio management, enabling real-time monitoring and data-driven decision-making to optimize their portfolio companies' performance.

Global Expansion of Private Equity Markets

The private equity landscape has witnessed a significant shift towards global expansion, with private equity firms increasingly looking beyond domestic markets to seek investment opportunities and diversify their portfolios. In this section, we explore the expanding global footprint of private equity and its implications.

1. Geographic Diversification:

Private equity firms are diversifying their portfolios by investing in companies located in different countries and regions. This geographic diversification aims to mitigate risks associated with overconcentration in a single market and provides exposure to diverse economic cycles.

2. Emerging Markets:

Emerging markets have become a focal point for private equity investment. These markets offer attractive growth prospects, untapped consumer bases, and opportunities in sectors such as technology, healthcare, and infrastructure. Private equity firms are actively seeking investments in regions like Southeast Asia, Latin America, and Africa.

3. Cross-Border Deals:

Cross-border deals are increasingly common in the private equity space. Firms are collaborating with international partners and investing in companies with global operations. Cross-border transactions enable access to new markets and expertise, fostering innovation and growth.

4. Regional Expertise:

Private equity firms are building expertise in specific regions, leveraging local knowledge and networks. This regional specialization helps in identifying unique investment opportunities, navigating regulatory nuances, and establishing strong partnerships with local businesses.

5. Industry Focus:

Global expansion also includes a focus on specific industries with international appeal. Private equity firms invest in sectors with global relevance, such as technology, healthcare, renewable energy, and e-commerce.

6. Infrastructure and Mega Projects:

Investment in large-scale infrastructure projects, such as transportation, energy, and telecommunications, is on the rise. Private equity firms are attracted to the long-term revenue streams and stability offered by these projects.

7. Global Fundraising:

Private equity firms are raising capital from investors worldwide, further fueling their ability to invest globally. This global fundraising approach allows firms to access a broader pool of capital to deploy in various markets.

8. Regulatory Considerations:

Navigating diverse regulatory environments is a challenge in global expansion. Private equity firms must stay well-versed in local regulations, tax implications, and compliance requirements to ensure seamless cross-border investments.

Practical Insight:

Apex Capital, a private equity firm specializing in technology investments, exemplifies the global expansion trend. They have strategically expanded their investment portfolio to include technology companies with international reach. Apex Capital leverages its global network to identify promising startups and scale-ups across different continents.

The Future of Private Equity: Challenges and Opportunities

The future of private equity promises both challenges and opportunities as the industry continues to evolve and adapt to a rapidly changing global landscape. In this section, we explore the key factors that will shape the future of private equity.

1. Evolving Regulatory Environment:

Private equity faces an evolving regulatory landscape as governments worldwide introduce new rules and reporting requirements. Firms must navigate complex compliance measures, tax regulations, and ESG mandates. Compliance with these regulations will be essential to maintaining trust and transparency.

2. Increased ESG Integration:

Environmental, Social, and Governance (ESG) considerations will play an increasingly significant role in private equity. Firms that effectively integrate ESG principles into their investment strategies will have a competitive edge, but they must also manage the challenges of measuring and reporting on ESG impact.

3. Technology and Data Analytics:

The integration of advanced technology and data analytics will continue to transform private equity operations. Artificial intelligence, machine learning, and big data will enhance investment decision-making, due diligence, and portfolio management. Firms that embrace these technologies will gain a substantial advantage.

4. Global Expansion:

Global expansion will remain a central theme in private equity, with firms seeking opportunities in emerging markets and diversifying their portfolios across regions and industries. International partnerships and cross-border deals will continue to drive growth.

5. Impact Investing:

Impact investing, focusing on both financial returns and positive societal and environmental outcomes, will gain momentum. Private equity firms will increasingly target investments that align with specific ESG goals, attracting socially conscious investors.

6. Competition for Quality Deals:

As private equity becomes more popular among institutional and retail investors, competition for high-quality deals will intensify. Firms will need to differentiate themselves through industry expertise, operational improvements, and value creation strategies.

7. Portfolio Company Resilience:

The ability of portfolio companies to weather economic downturns and disruptions will be critical. Private equity firms will focus on enhancing portfolio company resilience through risk mitigation strategies and robust crisis management plans.

8. Investor Expectations:

Investor expectations for transparency, ESG integration, and responsible investing will continue to rise. Private equity firms must meet these expectations to attract and retain capital.

9. Exit Strategies:

Exit strategies will evolve, with more emphasis on IPOs, special purpose acquisition companies (SPACs), and strategic sales. Firms will need to adapt to changing exit dynamics and market conditions.

10. Talent and Diversity:

Attracting and retaining top talent will be crucial for private equity firms. Fostering diversity and inclusion within the industry will also become a priority, reflecting societal and investor demands.

Practical Insight:

Vista Capital, a forward-thinking private equity firm, is actively preparing for the future by focusing on technology-driven investments, ESG integration, and impact initiatives. They recognize that staying ahead of industry trends and investor expectations positions them for long-term success.

In conclusion, the future of private equity holds both challenges and opportunities. While regulatory complexities and competition intensify, private equity firms that embrace technology, ESG principles, and global expansion will thrive. The industry's ability to adapt to evolving investor preferences and societal demands will determine its success in the dynamic landscape ahead.

Don't miss out!

Visit the website below and you can sign up to receive emails whenever Alex Thompson publishes a new book. There's no charge and no obligation.

https://books2read.com/r/B-A-FEPY-HZWOC

BOOKS 2 READ

Connecting independent readers to independent writers.

Also by Alex Thompson

Alex on Finance

Financial Freedom Roadmap - Achieving Early Retirement through the FIRE Movement

The Art of Strategic Innovation

Beyond Cash - The Evolution of Digital Payment Systems and the Future of Money

Preserving Wealth in Inflationary Times - Strategies for Protecting Your Financial Future

Standalone

Side Hustle Success: Unlocking Your Entrepreneurial Potential

Side Hustle Success: The Ultimate Guide to Passive and Financial Freedom

Mastering the Markets: Advanced Trading Strategies for Success and Ethical Trading Practices

Financial Fortitude

Mastering the Art of Upselling

The Financial Bullet Blueprint

Investing Demystified: A Beginner's Guide to Building Wealth in the Stock Market

Real Estate Riches: Building Wealth through Property Investment

How To Succeed as a Freelancer

Navigating Complex Waters: Advanced Strategies in Portfolio Management
Behavioral Finance and Investor Psychology
Leading with Empathy: Harnessing Emotional Intelligence for Effective Leadership
Financial Independence
Thriving Within Your Means: A Guide to Affordable Living
Algorithmic Trading: Navigating the Digital Frontier
Navigating Alternative Investments
Navigating the Behavioral Finance Landscape
Unlocking the Power of Derivatives
Mastering International Finance
Quantitative Finance and Risk Modeling
Sustainable and ESG Investing
Derivatives Dynamics: Navigating Risk and Innovation
Options Mastery: Navigating the Financial Frontier
Portfolio Mastery: Navigating the Financial Art and Science
Ethics in Hedge Funds: Navigating the Moral Compass of Finance
Structured Finance: Navigating Innovation, Sustainability and Ethics
Commodity Trading: Navigating Markets, Sustainability, and Innovation
Ethical Valuation: Navigating the Future of Startup Investments
Navigating Financial Risk: Strategies for a Dynamic World
Navigating the New Frontier: Understanding Market Microstructure in the Digital Age
Mastering Mergers and Acquisitions: Strategies, Successes and Lessons
Mastering Real Estate Investment: Strategies, Trends and Success Stories
Navigating Investor Behavior: Insights from Behavioral Finance
Private Equity Horizons: Navigating Opportunities and Shaping the Future

www.ingramcontent.com/pod-product-compliance
Lightning Source LLC
LaVergne TN
LVHW022103200926
848481LV00003B/1050